TOMCAT FURY

A COMBAT HISTORY OF THE F-14

MIKE GUARDIA

From *Debrief: A Complete History of US Aerial Engagements, 1981 to the Present* by Craig Brown. Used by permission of Schiffer Publishing. Any third-party use of this material, outside of this publication, is prohibited. Interested parties must apply directly to Schiffer Publishing for permission.

From *Libyan Air Wars, Volumes 1-3*, by Tom Cooper. Used by permission of Helion & Company. Any third-party use of this material, outside of this publication, is prohibited. Interested parties must apply directly to Helion & Company for permission.

From *Iranian F-14 Tomcat Units in Combat*, by Tom Cooper and Farzad Bishop. Used by permission of Osprey Publishing. Any third-party use of this material, outside of this publication, is prohibited. Interested parties must apply directly to Osprey Publishing for permission.

From *F-14 Tomcat Units of Operation Enduring Freedom and F-14 Tomcat Units of Operation Iraqi Freedom* by Tony Holmes. Used by permission of Osprey Publishing. Any third-party use of this material, outside of this publication, is prohibited. Interested parties must apply directly to Osprey Publishing for permission.

From *Grumman F-14 Tomcat Owner's Workshop Manual* by Tony Holmes. Used by permission of Haynes Publishing UK. Any third-party use of this material, outside of this publication, is prohibited. Interested parties must apply directly to Haynes Publishing for permission.

Published by Magnum Books
PO Box 1661
Maple Grove, MN 55311

www.mikeguardia.com

ISBN-13: 978-0-9996443-3-1
ISBN-10: 0-9996443-3-5

For Marie and Melanie

Also by Mike Guardia:

American Guerrilla

Shadow Commander

Hal Moore: A Soldier Once…and Always

The Fires of Babylon

Crusader

Co-authored with Lt. General Harold G. Moore:

Hal Moore on Leadership

Contents

Introduction

For more than three decades, the Grumman F-14 Tomcat was the US Navy's premier carrier-based, multi-role fighter jet. From its harrowing combat missions over Libya to its appearance on the silver screen in movies like *Top Gun* and *Executive Decision*, the F-14 has become an icon of American air power. During its thirty-two years of naval service, the illustrious Tomcat garnered a reputation for its grit, glamor, and glory. Whether fulfilling the role of a high-seas interceptor, ground-attack aircraft, or an air superiority fighter, the F-14 was, without question, the US Navy's "jack-of-all-trades"—and a plane beloved by those who flew it.

The F-14 began its journey into the annals of naval history in 1974. Rolling off the assembly line at the Grumman Aerospace facility in Calverton, New York, the Tomcat entered service as a replacement for the McDonnell Douglas F-4 Phantom. With its state-of-the-art "swing wing" design, unmatched agility, and advanced avionics, the Tomcat seemed poised for a long and prosperous reign as the Navy's champion fighter jet. Aside from its operational versatility, the F-14 featured an advanced targeting system that could track up to twenty-four targets simultaneously and engage six of those targets at the same time.

The Tomcat made its operational debut in the seas over South Vietnam. As the fledgling and beleaguered republic fell to the Communists in April 1975, the F-14 Tomcat flew Combat Air Patrols and provided aerial cover to the heliborne evacuations from Saigon. In 1976, the F-14 conducted its first intercept of a Tupelov Tu-95 "Bear"—the Soviet Navy's premiere heavy bomber and reconnaissance aircraft. These intercepts became a recurring episode during the latter decades of the Cold War, ensuring that the Soviet bombers did not venture into American airspace or come within striking distance of the carrier groups at sea.

American Tomcats first proved their mettle in combat over the Gulf of Sidra. In August 1981, during a routine Combat Air Patrol off the northern coast of Libya, two F-14s from Squadron VF-41 "Black Aces" were engaged by a pair of Sukhoi Su-22 "Fitters" from the Libyan Air Force. Within minutes, however, both Tomcats had skillfully downed the Libyan bandits with a pair of AIM-9L Sidewinder missiles.

The F-14 Tomcat continued its illustrious service into the 1980s, much of it during the bombing campaigns against Libya, but also during the contingency operations in Lebanon, Grenada, and the infamous *Achille Lauro* Incident of 1985. Although the F-14 quickly rose to prominence as a symbol of American air power, it was the Islamic Republic of Iran who made the most extensive use of the F-14 in combat.

Today, Iran is the only foreign operator of the F-14 and it remains the only country in the world with an active Tomcat fleet. Once America's strongest ally in the Middle East, Iran solicited weapons from the US, hoping to achieve parity with its neighbor Iraq. Wanting to counter the Iraqis' latest-generation MiGs, the Shah of Iran needed something of comparable or greater value. Having been a pilot himself, the Shah was dedicated to making the Iranian Air Force the strongest in the Middle East. Working with Grumman and the Pentagon, the Shah negotiated a $2 billion contract for eighty F-14s, along with a full stock of replacement parts and hundreds of newly-built Phoenix missiles. This F-14 contract was, at the time, the highest-value single sale of US military equipment to a foreign power. Throughout its service in Iran's military, the F-14 garnered an impressive combat record during the Iran-Iraq War.

The F-14 continued its remarkable run in US service throughout the 1990s and well into the mid-2000s. During Operation Desert Storm, the US Navy saw many of its F-14s relegated to supporting roles—primarily strike escort missions and reconnaissance fly-bys. It was during Desert Storm that the F-14 suffered its only loss in combat. This loss, however, was partially mitigated by the Tomcat becoming the first fighter in American history to shoot down an enemy helicopter. Following the terrorist attacks of September 11, 2001, the F-14 Tomcat led some of the inaugural strikes against al-Qaeda and the Taliban during the opening stages of Operation Enduring Freedom.

The US Navy retired the F-14 from active service in September 2006—its final combat mission having occurred seven months earlier in support of Operation Iraqi Freedom. Despite the Tomcat's hard-earned reputation, acclaim, and ubiquity, however, there has never been a full combat history of the F-14 covered in one volume…until now.

Tomcat Fury examines the illustrious history of the F-14, discussing the plane's emergence, evolution, and its harrowing combat saga. From the Gulf of Sidra to the skies over Afghanistan, the Tomcat's legacy is one of unparalleled grace and formidability.

Design, Development, and Initial Deployment

I n the spring of 1973, the USS *Enterprise*—America's premiere aircraft carrier—began its long journey home from Vietnam. Throughout eight years of conflict, the "Big E," had deployed five times to the Southeast Pacific—launching more than 12,000 combat sorties. Now, in the wake of the Paris Peace Accords, it seemed that the war in Vietnam had finally come to an end. President Nixon had promised to end the war by achieving a so-called "peace with honor." Time, however, would prove him wrong. But

The McDonnell-Douglas F-4 Phantom II. In the skies over Vietnam, the F-4 Phantom was a formidable foe to the Communist North Vietnamese. However, by the end of the 1960s, the airplane had become obsolete in the face of the newer-generation Soviet MiGs. Grumman's F-14 Tomcat would eventually become the Phantom's replacement. (US Air Force)

The experimental F-111B in flight over Long Island, 1965. The F-111B was an early contender for the US Navy's next-generation carrier-based fighter. However, the plane's girth and its numerous design flaws rendered it unsuitable for carrier operations. Only seven airframes were built before the program was cancelled. (US Navy)

for the sailors, pilots, and naval aircrews aboard the *Enterprise*, the more pressing matter was how to reconfigure their ship to accommodate the Navy's newest fighter jet. Indeed, as the "Big E" docked into the Puget Sound Naval Shipyard, she began refitting her flight decks and aviation bays for the Grumman F-14 Tomcat.

From the outset of Vietnam, the McDonnell Douglas F-4 Phantom II had been the top fighter-interceptor for the US Navy, Air Force, and Marine Corps. This vaunted two-seat, twin-engine fighter had enjoyed a multi-faceted service life as both an air superiority and ground-attack aircraft. Whether escorting bombers, conducting aerial reconnaissance, or engaging in air-to-air combat, the F-4 provided an impressive *tour de force* from any angle. At more than 5,000 units built, the F-4 Phantom II still holds the record for the largest production run of any American supersonic fighter.

Despite its ubiquity, however, the F-4 Phantom had rapidly grown obsolete in the face of modern Soviet aircraft. In the summer of 1967, for example, the Soviets unveiled the new MiG-23 and MiG-25, both of which were purportedly capable of outmaneuvering any jet within the NATO arsenal. In the skies over Vietnam, the F-4, though solidly victorious, had nevertheless shown its vulnerabilities. Indeed, its biggest liability was its weight burden—carrying a gross weight of more than 40,000 pounds. Although its twin General Electric J79 engines provided ample airspeed, the F-4 was not particularly agile compared to the lighter-weight MiG-17s and MiG-21s.

Of seemingly greater concern were the telltale plumes that the J79 engine emitted during flight. This made the F-4 Phantom easy to detect among enemy aircrews and anti-aircraft personnel (ironic considering the airplane's "Phantom" nickname). Although stealth technology was still on the horizon, American pilots nevertheless preferred an aircraft whose flight patterns weren't so easily detectable.

Fortunately, for these seasoned F-4 pilots, a new fighter jet was already under development. Under the auspices of Defense Secretary Robert J. McNamara, the Tactical Fighter Experimental (TFX) program called for a joint-service aircraft that would fulfill the operational requirements of the US Navy and Air Force. Accordingly, the Air Force needed a long-range fighter-bomber (not dissimilar to the F-100 series of the 1950s) while the Navy needed an agile, long-range fighter capable of air-to-air combat while defending the parent fleet. Thus, on September 1, 1961, McNamara directed there to be a "single aircraft for both the Air Force tactical mission and the Navy fleet air defense mission."

The General Dynamics Corporation, a powerhouse in the aerospace and defense industries, won the initial bid for their prototype: The F-111B. Seven prototypes were constructed, the first of which took its maiden flight on May 18, 1965. While the airframe was sturdy and its performance sufficient, it nevertheless failed to address the shortcomings of the F-4 Phantom. At more than 75,000 pounds, the F-111B far exceeded the maximum operational weight of the F-4. Moreover, the F-111B's size and weight had rendered it unsuitable for carrier operations. To be certain, the plane was fast, but its top speed of Mach 2.2 was still below the standard for which the Navy and Air Force had deemed acceptable. To make matters worse, the cockpit design made for poor visibility of the surrounding airspace. During Congressional hearings for the F-111B, Vice Admiral Thomas F. Connolly, then-Deputy Chief of Naval Operations for Air Warfare, famously quipped to Senator John Stennis:

"There isn't enough power in all Christendom to make that airplane what we want!"

The F-111B program was subsequently cancelled in May 1968, although it's parallel-produced stablemate, the F-111A survived to become a multi-purpose aircraft for the US Air Force.

Grumman's F-14A Tomcat prototype, which made its inaugural flight on December 21, 1970. Following four additional years of testing and evaluation, the F-14 officially entered service in 1974. (US Navy)

The cockpit of an F–14A Tomcat, shown here in 1980. (NASA)

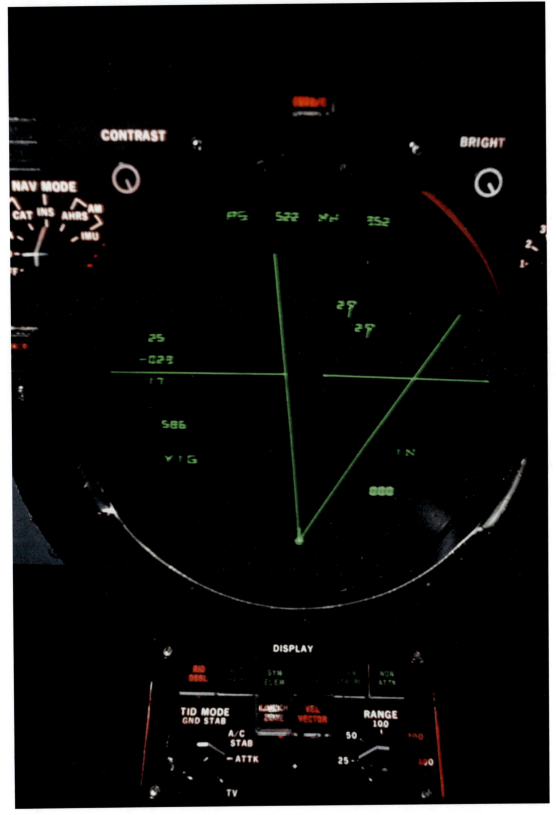

The Radar Intercept Officer (RIO) sat in the rear of the cockpit. The RIO's station featured the AWG-9 radar system (pictured here), which allowed the crew to track multiple targets and guide the AIM-54 Phoenix missile. (US Department of Defense)

With such a poor assessment of the F-111B, some within the naval aviation community discussed the possibility of upgrading the F-4. However, defense planners soon realized that even with a multi-million-dollar redesign, the F-4 still paled in comparison to the forthcoming generation of MiGs and Sukhois. Come what may, the F-4 Phantom II simply wasn't agile enough to contend with its anticipated adversaries.

Thus, on June 21, 1968, Naval Air Systems Command issued a "Request for Proposals" to all major companies within the aerospace industry. The specifications called for a two-seat, twin-engine, carrier-based fighter-interceptor capable of firing the AIM-7 Sparrow, AIM-9 Sidewinder, and the forthcoming AIM-54 Phoenix missiles. In what became known as the Naval Fighter Experimental (VFX) program, US aerospace giants including Grumman, General Dynamics, McDonnell, and North American submitted designs for the prototype competition. Each of the contenders had had a long and successful history in the realm of military aerospace. Grumman, for example, had fielded the F6F Hellcat and TBF Avenger— both of which had been staples of the Pacific Theater during World War II. Grumman's most recent success was the A-6 Intruder, a subsonic attack aircraft that had been well-received by Naval and Marine Corps air squadrons. North American's P-51 Mustang had dominated the skies over the European Theater, while their T-6 Texan had been the standard trainer for the US Army Air Forces. General Dynamics, though a relative newcomer to the world of aviation, had been a key player in fielding the F-106 interceptor and the B-58 bomber. McDonnell (prior to its merger with Douglas Aircraft), had produced the F2H Banshee, one of the primary carrier-based fighters of the Korean War.

Three Tomcat prototypes in flight near Calverton, New York, 1972. Each of the three aircraft is demonstrating the different wing configurations that the F-14 could achieve through its variable sweep-wing design. Via the on-board computer, or manually via the pilot, the F-14 could adjust the position of its wings to accommodate different speeds and gravitational forces. (National Museum of Naval Aviation)

A Tomcat displays its AIM-54 Phoenix missiles. The AIM-54 was a long-range, radar-guided missile built exclusively for the F-14. The US Navy used the AIM-54 until 2004, retiring the missile two years before retiring the Tomcat itself. (US Navy)

Among the various contenders for the VFX program, only Grumman and McDonnell were selected for the final stakes. From the outset, however, Grumman had the upper hand. Having worked in conjunction with General Dynamics on the failed F-111B project, Grumman designers knew exactly what *not* to repeat. Accordingly, they knew that weight considerations were a primary concern. Thus, they designed an aircraft made from titanium, constructed through electron-beam welding. With an airframe containing forty-five machined parts and 100 separate welds, the Grumman prototype (simply named "303") was lighter, more agile, and could achieve greater acceleration than its McDonnell counterpart. Another improvement made to Grumman's 303 design was the inclusion of the AWG-9 radar system. The AWG-9 used a passive Infrared Search and Track (IRST) system that was gimbal-mounted on a chin pod, under the nose of the aircraft. The system could work independently or in conjunction with the on-board missile system. Thus, it gave pilots the ability to scan one sector of the surrounding airspace via radar, while scanning a different sector via IRST. Simultaneously, the AWG-9 created a windfall for the airframe's weight requirement, as it lowered the volume inside the aircraft from 46 cubic feet to 30 cubic feet.

Grumman also focused on how to maximize the plane's agility. For close combat and high maneuverability, Grumman gave its fighter a variable-sweep wing design. These adjustable wings (or "swing wings," as they were known), could be swept back or pushed forward to accommodate different speeds at different altitudes, and against

An F-14 from Squadron VF-111 armed with the AIM-9 Sidewinder missile. Aside from the AIM-54, the Tomcat frequently carried the AIM-7 Sparrow and AIM-9 Sidewinder as part of its combat load. (US Navy)

different g-forces. These "swing wings" would, ideally, have multiple settings and could sweep seamlessly between positions without affecting the plane's overall stability. This revolutionary design not only improved the fighter's agility, it also provided a rapid means of acceleration. In fact, the Tomcat's sweep-variable wings were one of its greatest assets. The "swing wing" system could be controlled either by the on-board Central Air Data Computer (CADC) or manually by the pilot. The CADC was able to calibrate and maintain the optimum lift-to-drag ratio as the F-14's airspeed increased or decreased. In flight, the variation of the wing position could be anywhere from 20-68 degrees. When parked on the aircraft carrier, however, the wings could be pulled back to 75 degrees, thereby permitting more space on the flight deck.

After Grumman and McDonnel submitted their designs for the VFX program, Grumman's 303 model won the final competition. The US Department of Defense subsequently awarded Grumman the final contract on January 14, 1969. Production called for six operational prototypes and 463 production aircraft. Thus, as Grumman began production of this next-generation fighter, the VFX officially became the "F-14."

Meanwhile, Chief of Naval Operations, Admiral Thomas Moorer, articulated the critical nature of the Navy's newest fighter jet. Like most flag officers, Moorer was aware that American military aircraft had fallen behind their Soviet counterparts. In a 1969 memorandum, he addressed the superior performance of eight new Soviet fighters—including the MiG-23, MiG-25, and Su-22. "We must have a new fighter," he said, "superior in air combat to [current] and postulated Soviet fighters, for close-in visual encounters and for stand-off, all-weather conditions. In addition, the new fighter must be able to defeat enemy air threats to naval forces: bombers and missiles."

With production of the F-14 underway, Moorer emphasized the characteristics that this newest naval fighter needed to have. He wrote that "the F-14…will be highly maneuverable…it will also have a higher degree of reliability, maneuverability, and weapons versatility than we have ever achieved. The key to a good fighter is to have a balanced, well-proportioned aircraft with a good thrust-to-weight ratio to provide high speed, good range, outstanding acceleration, and the aerodynamic characteristics to ensure the best possible maneuverability. These attributes are essential to beat the enemy."

Likewise, Vice Admiral Thomas F. Connolly, the aforementioned Deputy Chief of Naval Operations for Air Warfare, championed the F-14 over the ill-fated F-111B and he eventually became the F-14 project manager. Indeed, it was Moorer's and Connolly's involvement that gave the F-14 its nickname: the "Tomcat." Grumman also had a history of naming their fighter aircraft after felines (F6F Hellcat and F8F Bearcat, for example). Thus, the plane to which they had jokingly called "Tom's Cat," officially became the F-14 Tomcat.

During the initial contract development, naval aviation planners determined that there needed to be multiple variants of the F-14, developed and delivered on staggered timetables over the next decade. The first of these variants, the "F-14A," needed to be

On the flight deck of the USS *Enterprise*, a brand-new F-14 stands ready for its first operational deployment, 1974. This Tomcat belongs to Squadron VF-1, one of the two inaugural Tomcat squadrons. (US Navy)

operational by April 1973. The second variant, the "F-14B," would be equipped with a more powerful engine: the forthcoming Pratt & Whitney F401. Finally, "F-14C" variant would feature improved avionics and air-to-ground capabilities. The C-variant, however, did not enter production—yielding instead to the F-14D.

Throughout this design process, some questioned the need (and associated costs) for fielding multiple variants. These skeptics proposed skipping the F-14A and simply waiting for the B variant to come online. Admiral Moorer, however, disagreed—stating that "proceeding by means of evolution from the F-14A to the F-14B reduces the risk and provides distinct and substantial savings in cost and time. It also provides flexibility to meet other military objectives. The F-14A represents a comparatively low-risk development program which would produce, at an early time, an advanced fighter fully capable of countering the threat. Stopping the F-14A program and proceeding only with the F-14B would result in additional program costs of $340 million."

After winning the contract for the F-14, Grumman aggressively expanded its Calverton (Long Island) facility for evaluating the aircraft. Indeed, much of the initial testing took place over Long Island Sound. To save time (and possibly stave off interference from the Secretary of Defense), the Navy elected not to build a prototype and thus moved directly into full-scale development.

The F-14 Tomcat made its inaugural test flight on December 21, 1970—a mere twenty-two months after Grumman won the VFX contract. Conducting this maiden flight was Grumman's chief test pilot, Robert Smythe, and the project test pilot, William Miller. In order to replicate anticipated fleet conditions, the Tomcat's wings were kept in

A Tomcat from Squadron VF-1 is hooked up to a catapult for launching from the flight deck of the USS *Enterprise*—March 17, 1975. Within weeks, the *Enterprise* would be diverted to the South China Sea, where its Tomcats would provide aerial cover for the evacuation of Saigon. (US Navy)

Fighters from Squadron VF-1 and VF-2, the first operational Tomcat squadrons, line the decks of the *Enterprise* as the carrier lumbers onward into the Pacific. (US Navy)

the forward position while the aircraft carried four mock AIM-7 Sparrow missiles.

This inaugural flight consisted of nothing more than two laps made around the Calverton airfield, but Smythe and Miller had nevertheless demonstrated the airworthiness of the new F-14. With the Navy's desire for immediate delivery, Grumman maintained a rapid evaluation schedule over the next few years, completing dozens of test flights and ordnance trials. By early 1974, the Navy had begun shipping the F-14 to Bremerton, Washington, where, in the confines of the Puget Sound Naval Shipyard, the USS *Enterprise* lay waiting to accept the new fighter jet.

Although Grumman had seemingly achieved its goal to develop a carrier-based fighter with air superiority and long-range intercept capabilities, the initial F-14s were not without their drawbacks. For example, the F-14A's engine—the Pratt & Whitney TF30—was terribly underpowered for its airframe. Although the TF30 met the Navy's airspeed requirements (Mach 2.34), the engine gave the Tomcat a thrust-to-weight ratio of only *0.64*—much lower than that of the F-4 Phantom. Indeed, many Tomcat pilots derisively called the TF30 "The Little Engine That Couldn't." Aside from the engine's low performance, the TF30 was also prone to mechanical failures. In fact, for all F-14s that were powered by the TF30, more than 28% of accidents were caused by engine failure.

An F-14 Tomcat from Squadron VF-2 "Bounty Hunters" launches from the catapult aboard the USS *Enterprise* on April 28, 1975. As South Vietnam fell to the Communists, Tomcats from VF-1 and VF-2 flew Combat Air Patrols during what would be called Operation Frequent Wind—an evacuation of American personnel from South Vietnam. (US Navy)

Fortunately, latter-day variants of the F-14 (including the F-14A Plus, F-14B, and F-14D) were upgraded to receive the General Electric F-110 engine. A significant upgrade from its Pratt & Whitney predecessor, the F-110 was a better fit for the airframe. In fact, the F-110 could produce up to 30,200 pounds of thrust—a significant improvement over the TF30's maximum thrust of only 20,900 pounds.

Engine woes aside, however, the Tomcat pilots celebrated their plane's numerous other features. The bubble canopy, for example, provided great visibility and was spacious enough to accommodate two tandem ejection seats. The controls were ergonomically friendly and the plane handled well during aerial maneuvers. At the front of the plane sat the pilot and, behind him, the Radar Intercept Officer (RIO). The RIO's responsibilities were navigation, communication, and operating the on-board weapons systems. Thus, in aerial combat, both the pilot and RIO would share responsibility for the engagement.

Tomcat pilots also took stock in the AWG-9 radar—an all-weather, multi-mode Doppler system. It was the most advanced radar system of its day and could simultaneously track up to twenty-four targets at a range of 195 miles. This was a huge leap forward from the F-4 Phantom. The AWG-9 was also capable of separating the surface of the Earth from low-lying aircraft, giving the crew better visuals of their intended targets. While tracking these twenty-four targets, the AWG-9 could engage six of them at once, launching the AIM-54 Phoenix missiles. Thus, the F-14 Tomcat became the first fighter jet with the ability to engage multiple targets simultaneously. The AIM-54 Phoenix missiles were specifically designed for long range air-to-air combat, and they were carried aboard the F-14 in clusters of six, each weighing 1,000 pounds. Due to weight restrictions, however, many F-14s carried a mix of Sparrow, Sidewinder, and Phoenix missiles.

For aerial engagements deemed too close for missiles, the Tomcat came equipped with a 20mm M61 Vulcan autocannon. The Vulcan was an air-cooled, six-barrel, rotary gun capable of delivering 6,000 rounds per minute. However, due to weight considerations, the F-14 typically carried only 675 rounds. The M61 was mounted internally in the forward section of the fuselage on the port side.

By the fall of 1973, the F-14 was ready for operational fleet use. By most accounts, the US Navy felt that the Tomcat had satisfied their requirements. Indeed, the plane had a powerful radar, long-range intercept capabilities, automated swing wings, good maneuverability, and could presumably keep pace with the current lineup of Soviet fighters. Still awaiting the delivery of these newly-constructed jets, the USS *Enterprise* continued upgrading its facilities at breakneck speed. These renovations included expanding two of the carrier's four jet blast deflectors. Finally, after more than six months of retooling and refinishing the *Enterprise*, the first F-14 Tomcat launched from her flight decks on March 18, 1974.

The pilots in these initial carrier flights were from fighter Squadron VF-1 "Wolfpack" and Squadron VF-2 "Bounty Hunters." Both squadrons had been established at Naval Air Station Miramar in 1972, specifically to receive the new F-14. Thus, when the "Big E" left Puget Sound on its seventh deployment to the Pacific in September 1974, it made history as the first carrier to do so with the F-14 Tomcat aboard.

Having completed its mission during Operation Frequent Wind, the *Enterprise* and her contingent of F-14s make the long journey home. Although the F-14 had not exchanged fire with any hostile aircraft, the mission in Southeast Asia proved the Tomcat's capabilities under actual fleet conditions. (US Navy)

During its initial months at sea, the *Enterprise* conducted various training exercises and assisted with humanitarian efforts in Port Louis, Mauritius. However, this routine deployment took an unexpected turn in April 1975. Following the US withdrawal from Vietnam in 1973, the Paris Peace Accords called for a permanent demarcation of North and South Vietnam. The North Vietnamese, however, had no intention of abiding by the accords. When Hanoi was certain that the US would not intervene, the Communists invaded South Vietnam in the spring of 1975.

In response, ARVN troops mounted an unsuccessful defense before retreating through Hue, Danang, and finally Da Lat. With the North Vietnamese closing in on Saigon, the South Vietnamese forces made their last stand at the Battle of Xuan Loc. As Communist tanks rolled into Saigon on the morning of April 30, 1975, the South Vietnamese government finally surrendered.

As the Communists tightened their noose around South Vietnam, however, the USS *Enterprise* got the call to assist the evacuation of American civilians from Saigon. In what became known as Operation Frequent Wind, the F-14 provided aerial cover for the hasty rescue, evacuating civilians from the wrath of North Vietnam.

The rescue operation was a multi-pronged approach, including evacuations by sea and air. As it turned out, naval helicopters from the US Seventh Fleet performed most of the evacuations—making Frequent Wind the largest helicopter rescue mission in history. The plan was for the American helicopters to land at the US Embassy and Defense Attaché Office (DAO) in Saigon, and shuttle evacuees to US naval ships waiting in the South China Sea. By helicopter, a total of 6,968 Americans and Vietnamese were evacuated. Throughout the operation, the United States accounted for 138,869 South Vietnamese refugees.

F-14s flying from the decks of the *Enterprise*, meanwhile, provided air support for the slower aircraft and ground troops handling the transport of US and South Vietnamese personnel. During the operation, the F-14s from Squadrons VF-1 and VF-2, along with the attack groups from the USS *Coral Sea*, fell under the operational control of Task Force 77.

After two arduous days of round-trip flights, the final helicopter left the roof of the US Embassy at 7:53 AM on April 30, 1975—just as Saigon fell to the North Vietnamese. And although there had been no combat for the F-14 during Frequent Wind, the Navy pilots and RIOs felt confident in the capabilities of their new fighter jet. They had provided the necessary aerial cover and demonstrated a show of force that the Communists dared not engage. Although Operation Frequent Wind signaled the end of the Navy's involvement in Vietnam, it was nevertheless a proving ground for the latest and greatest asset in US naval aviation—the F-14 Tomcat.

Variants

From 1969-91, a total of 712 F-14s were built. More than 160 were destroyed in accidents. Throughout its service life, the Tomcat had three operational variants, the first of which was the F-14A. The US Navy received 478 F-14As in the early 1970s, while the Imperial

Tomcats intercepting a Soviet Tu-95 "Bear" on the high seas. The Soviet Navy and Soviet Air Force frequently sent their long-range reconnaissance planes to the frontiers of American airspace. On other occasions, these Soviet planes would shadow American carrier groups at sea. Ensuring that these Tu-95s did not venture too close to the carrier group, American F-14s would intercept the offending planes and escort them from the area. These intercepts were a common occurrence throughout the 1970s–80s.
(US Navy)

An F-14 Tomcat from VF-101 after landing aboard the USS *Independence*, June 1979. (US Navy)

Air Force of Iran received 79.

The F-14A received the first of its many upgrades in March 1987, with the development of the F-14A *Plus*. This "Plus" variant replaced the maligned TF30 engine with the F-110 engine from General Electric. The F-14A Plus also received the upgraded ALR-67 Radar Homing and Warning system, improving the pilot's and RIO's real-time awareness of the battlespace. Grumman retained much of the on-board avionics, including the AWG-9 radar. The F-14A Plus was later re-designated the "F-14B." From 1987-91, Grumman built a total of 38 new F-14A Plus, while 48 F-14A base models were upgraded into B variants. In the late 1990s, 67 F-14Bs received upgrades to their airframes along with improved avionics systems. These modified versions became known simply as the "F-14B Upgrade." The F-14C variant never entered production, but many of its concepts were recycled into the F-14D.

The F-14D was the final variant—known as the "Super Tomcat." The F-14D was first delivered in 1991. Carrying the improved General Electric F-110 engines, the F-14D also featured improved avionics. The legacy AWG-9 was replaced with a newer and more powerful AN/APG-71 radar.

Other on-board systems for the F-14D included the Joint Tactical Information Distribution System (JTIDS). This system tracked the position, identity, and status of both friendly and enemy forces, in addition to providing information on weather and command updates.

Similar to the F-14B, the General Electric F-110 engine provided greater thrust and additional endurance for the F-14D. Conclusively, the F-110 gave the Super Tomcat a sixty-percent greater striking range and one-third more time on station. The increased thrust also allowed the F-14D to perform carrier launches without going to full afterburner.

Although the Super Tomcat was to be the definitive version of the F-14, not all squadrons received the D-variant. In 1989, then-Defense Secretary Dick Cheney opted for a $25 million modernization program, upgrading the existing fleet of F-14s to the Super Tomcat, D-variant specifications. According to Secretary Cheney, this modernization program would cost less than half of the purchase price for newly-built F-14Ds. As a compromise, however, Congress decided not to shut production down of the F-14D and funded the production of 55 aircraft. A total of 37 new aircraft were eventually built, while 18 F-14A models were upgraded to D-variants. These new variants were given to a handful of Tomcat squadrons, including Squadron VF-2 "Bounty Hunters", VF-11 "Red Rippers", and VF-31 "Tomcatters."

Variably, the F-14D was also known as the "Bombcat" for its ability to deliver air-to-ground munitions as an attack aircraft. Although the Tomcat had been conceived and developed with a ground attack capability in mind, it was a long time before the air-to-ground capability came to fruition. This change in functionality, however, was critical to the Tomcat's survival in a post-Cold War era. Amidst the draconian defense budgets of the 1990s, and the changing nature of modern warfare, the F-14 needed to evolve from a fighter-interceptor to a multi-role attack aircraft. While this change was necessary to keep the F-14 in the sky, it was a hard pill for many to swallow. Several fighter pilots had enjoyed the panache and mystique of the "fighter jock" culture—and did not want to be lumped into the same category as reconnaissance or bomber pilots.

According to James "Puck" Howe, a Navy Strike Fighter Tactics Instructor:

"When I was a young student in VF-101 in the early 1990s, the Tomcat was just starting to develop the air-to-ground capability that had been inherent in the aeroplane since its creation. Looking back, it's pretty funny, as we didn't really have any idea what we were doing. It wasn't exactly giving a loaded gun to a child, but it was close. Moreover, no one really seemed too serious or too happy about the F-14's potential to become a 'strike fighter.' We were purebred fighter pilots - stuck-up, arrogant, and shameless. We sang 'You've Lost that Loving Feeling' and made it look cool. Dropping bombs was for people who didn't make the cut. But our leadership kept telling us that a single-role aircraft would not last long in a newly cost-conscious Navy. If we didn't figure out bomb dropping, and quickly, the Tomcat was going to fade unceremoniously into oblivion."

Despite the Tomcat's popularity and its competitive edge among the world's fighter aircraft, however, Secretary Cheney seemed to be highly dismissive of the F-14. At one point, he called it "1960s technology" and even referred to the Tomcat as little more than a "jobs program." Towards the end of his tenure as the Secretary of Defense, Cheney had planned to replace the F-14 with a non-Grumman fighter—despite an appeal from the Secretary of the Navy for at least 132 additional F-14Ds. Nevertheless, the F-14D and its sister variants continued to serve in the fleet until the Tomcat's retirement in 2006.

Throughout the 1990s, Grumman Aerospace proposed a few more versions of the

Super Tomcat. The first was a "Quick Strike" variant—featuring advanced navigational and targeting pods, along with enhanced ground-attack capabilities. It was intended to replace the rapidly-aging A-6 Intruder. Congress, however, was not impressed by the Quick Strike design, prompting Grumman to shift its attention to the "Super Tomcat 21."

Super Tomcat 21 was a proposed alternative to the fledgling Navy Advanced Tactical Fighter (NATF) program. The Super Tomcat 21 would have the same shape and body as the legacy Tomcat, but with upgraded capabilities, better avionics, new engines with increased fuel capacity, and modified control surfaces. The subsequent "Attack Super Tomcat 21" was a further-modified design that added attack capabilities via an Active Electronically-Scanned Array (AESA) radar.

Grumman's final attempt to reincarnate the legacy Tomcat was the Advanced Strike Fighter-14 (ASF-14). As Grumman's replacement for the NATF concept, the ASF-14 would resemble the legacy Tomcat in appearance, but incorporate newer technologies from the Air Force's Advanced Tactical Fighter (ATF) program. In the end, however, the Navy decided that the latter-day Tomcat redesigns would be too costly—and pursued the cheaper, lightweight F/A-18 Hornets to fulfill the joint fighter-attack role.

Gulf of Sidra Incident, 1981

By the dawn of the 1980s, the strength and capabilities of the F-14 Tomcat were known throughout the world. Following its debut in the skies over Southeast Asia, the Tomcat had earned its reputation as the most versatile carrier-based fighter in the world. As the final squadrons completed their transition to the F-14, the legend of the plane continued to grow as its encounters with Soviet aircraft became more frequent.

During the Cold War, the Soviet Navy and Air Force routinely sent their strategic

The intrepid crews of *Fast Eagle 102* and *Fast Eagle 107*, the two Tomcats from Squadron VF-41 who downed two Libyan Sukhoi Su-22s over the Gulf of Sidra in August 1981. Pictured from left to right are: Lieutenant David Venlet, Commander Henry Kleeman, Lieutenant Lawrence Muczynski, and Lieutenant (Junior Grade) James Anderson. (US Navy)

Six RH-53D Sea Stallion helicopters fly over the USS *Nimitz* in preparation for "Operation Eagle Claw," the failed attempt to rescue American hostages in Iran, April 1980. Lieutenant Muczynski was onboard the *Nimitz*, serving with Squadron VF-41, when the carrier received orders to assist with Eagle Claw. In the foreground are two F-14 Tomcats from Squadron VF-84 "Jolly Rogers," whom as part of Air Carrier Wing 8, flew alongside VF-41 during the Gulf of Sidra incident the following year. (US Navy)

aircraft—notably the Tupolev Tu-95 bomber (NATO reporting name: "Bear")—to the frontiers of American airspace. Similarly, these probing flights often shadowed US aircraft carriers on maneuver. The purpose of the Tu-95 was simple: by design, it was a heavy bomber comparable to the B-52. On the high seas, however, it found greater use as a long-range surveillance and reconnaissance aircraft. At the time, US defense policy stated that no Soviet aircraft could fly within 100 miles of the American coastline or an American carrier group at sea. However, in the ongoing game of brinksmanship, the Soviets continued to push the boundaries of America's defense posture. Indeed, the Tu-95 (among other Soviet aircraft) was a frequent visitor to US outposts. But whenever a Tu-95 vectored too close, a flight of Tomcats scrambled to intercept—with orders to guide the prowling aircraft back to a safe distance.

Most of these encounters with Soviet reconnaissance flights passed without incident. Some encounters were even humorous, as the pilots of either aircraft would make faces at one another or exchange colorful hand gestures. Nevertheless, these airborne intercepts had garnered the attention of allies and adversaries alike.

Although the international community had taken notice of the F-14 during these intercept engagements, there had been no true assessment of how the plane would perform in combat. These speculations abruptly ended, however, on the morning of August 19, 1981—several miles off the coast of Libya.

In the southern Mediterranean Sea, the Gulf of Sidra was the focal point of a hotly-contested debate regarding maritime law. Indeed, the Gulf of Sidra had been a talking point within the international community since the rise of Muammar al-Gaddafi as Libya's leader. In 1973, Gaddafi declared the entire Gulf of Sidra as Libyan territorial water. Essentially, he had drawn a line from the mouth of the Gulf of Sidra (32'30"North Latitude) stretching from the city of Misurata on the east to Benghazi on the west. With the stroke of a pen, Gaddafi had laid claim to more than 150,000 square miles of the Mediterranean Sea. Any encroachment into the Gulf of Sidra, he added, would be seen as an act of aggression.

Most of the world, however, only recognized twelve miles from a country's shoreline as the limit for its territorial waters. Countering Libya's argument, the US referenced the 1958 Convention on the Territorial Sea and Contiguous Zone. Although Libya had not been a signator, the territorial sea convention nevertheless stated that a country could only include a coastal embayment in its territorial waters if it spanned 24 miles or less.

The Gulf of Sidra was 275 miles long.

An F-4 Phantom intercepts a Libyan MiG-23 over the Gulf of Sidra, August 1981. As Libyan leader Muammar al-Gaddafi ramped up his rhetoric regarding the nautical "Line of Death," his air force began intercepting more American planes over the Gulf of Sidra. Most of the interceptions, however, ended without confrontation. F-14 pilots like Kleeman and Muczynski recalled encountering a number of MiG-23s, MiG-25s, and Mirage F1s. (US Navy)

A Libyan Sukhoi Su-22. On August 19, 1981, two Su-22s from the Libyan Air Force engaged Kleeman's and Muczynski's F-14s over the Gulf of Sidra. From the outset, however, the dogfight was a mismatch. For even at maximum armament, the Su-22 could not match the F-14's firepower or maneuverability. (Chris Lofting)

Thus, because the Gulf of Sidra did not meet the convention's territorial guidelines, the United States refused to recognize what Gadaffi had declared as his "Line of Death." Undeterred by the international rhetoric, and a seemingly-outdated 1958 treaty, the Libyan leader proudly beat his chest and bragged that he would shoot down any US aircraft that vectored into the Gulf of Sidra.

Muammar al-Gaddafi had an unshakable confidence in Libya's Air Force. Given his close ties to the Soviet Union, and his recent acquisition of the latest Soviet-built fighter jets, one could hardly blame him. Like most world leaders, Gaddafi had watched the American folly in Vietnam, and he felt that the post-war US had become little more than a paper tiger. On tarmacs across Libya, Gaddafi's air force proudly displayed the newest Su-22 fighter-bombers, MiG-25 interceptors, and Tu-22 tactical bombers. These purchases, made in 1978, gave the Libyan Air Force approximately 100 aircraft capable of reaching Mach 3 at high altitudes.

Normally, the US would have no cause for concern over the mindless "saber-rattling" of a Third World dictator. However, Gaddafi's rhetoric was directly addressing the navigational exercises that the US Navy (and other seagoing fleets) had practiced for decades. Indeed, maneuvering on the high seas allowed blue-water navies the opportunity to hone their skills as wartime seafarers. For naval aviators, these navigational exercises gave them the ability to test-fire missiles and engage in mock dogfights under realistic fleet conditions. Thus, Libya's re-imaging of its territorial waters posed a direct challenge to the rights of international seagoing.

Under President Jimmy Carter, the US Navy had begun sending its battle groups into the Gulf of Sidra, both in defiance of Gaddafi's blustering and in defense of international maritime standards. The US State Department, meanwhile, announced that "oceans beyond the territorial seas are 'high seas' on which all nations enjoy freedom of navigation and overflights, including the right to engage in naval maneuvers."

In 1979, the United States launched an official Freedom of Navigation (FON) program to challenge positions such as Libya's. To this point, FON had simply been a tradition, carried out in practice by the US Navy and other maritime fleets. Going forward, however, FON would be an official program backed by authority of the US government and enforceable by the US military. It was through the official Freedom of Navigation program that, in August 1981, President Ronald Reagan approved military exercises in the Gulf of Sidra for the carriers USS *Forrestal* and USS *Nimitz*—the latter of which carried the F-14-based Fighter Squadron VF-41 "Black Aces." As part of the US Sixth Fleet, the *Forrestal* and *Nimitz* were sent to conduct maneuvers and provide a presence that Muammar al-Gaddafi couldn't ignore.

In the summer of 1981, Lieutenant Lawrence Muczynski (call sign: "Music") was enjoying his second fleet tour as a naval aviator. A 1976 Annapolis graduate, Muczynski had earned his wings at Naval Air Station (NAS) Kingsville and reported to VF-41 in 1979. At the time of his arrival, the squadron was preparing for a deployment to

An F-14 from Squadron VF-41 lands on the deck of the *Nimitz* after completing a Combat Air Patrol over the Mediterranean on August 1, 1981. By this time, Squadrons VF-41 and VF-84 had been intercepting a variety of Libyan aircraft, but none had initiated hostile fire. (US Navy)

the Mediterranean aboard the *Nimitz*. However, in the summer and fall of 1979, the world had focused its attention on the growing crisis in Iran. After nearly 2,000 years of monarchial rule, the House of the Shah was losing its grip on the Iranian people. Under the fiery rhetoric of the Ayatollah Khomeini, Iranians of every social stratum joined the revolution to end the reign of Shah Mohammed Reza Pahlavi. Although the United States had been Iran's closest Western ally, the Ayatollah focused his vitriol on America as the "Great Satan," declaring the US an enemy of the revolution. When his revolutionaries took hostages at the American embassy in Tehran, the USS *Nimitz* was promptly diverted to the Persian Gulf.

With VF-41 aboard, the *Nimitz* left the Mediterranean via the Straight of Gibraltar on January 2, 1980. Sailing around Africa, the *Nimitz* arrived at the edge of the Persian Gulf in a matter of weeks. As it turned out, the *Nimitz* would be the launching platform for the helicopters of Operation Eagle Claw—the ill-fated mission to rescue American hostages in Tehran. As Muczynski recalled, this deployment set the tone for the remainder of his active duty career.

After 144 days at sea without a single port call, the *Nimitz* returned to the United States in May 1980. Upon arriving at their home anchorage, VF-41 began to prepare for its next deployment to the Mediterranean, scheduled for summer 1981. Aware of Gaddafi's recent rhetoric regarding the Gulf of Sidra, the carrier task force issued a "Notice to Airmen and Mariners" (NOTAMS) regarding its upcoming maneuvers. Accordingly, the F-14 squadrons were to conduct an open-ocean missile shoot on August 18-19. The NOTAMS also outlined the operational area for the missile shoot—which included the Gulf of Sidra. "Even though it was a hundred miles out to sea," Muczynski said, "it did extend into the waters claimed by Libya...the infamous 'Line of Death'...so we expected them to challenge the exercise in some way."

The Rules of Engagement (ROE) for the exercise were very clear. No pilot could shoot without permission. Even if a pilot were fired upon, he would still have to obtain permission before returning fire.

To Lawrence Muczynski, however, this ROE seemed dangerous and counterproductive.

"In any engagement that lasts more than 60 seconds," he said, "your probability of getting shot increases exponentially." Luckily, the carrier task force modified its permission protocol prior to the deployment. "We could now be pre-cleared by our controllers to engage a specific target, and most importantly, if we were fired on, we could return fire, no questions asked." According to Muczynski, the initial ROE had been the result of excessive worry—the Navy was fearful of losing its EP-3 Orion, EA-6B Prowler, or E-2C Hawkeye planes to marauding Libyan fighters. Each of these planes provided a critical support function to the F-14s in flight. The EP-3 was a reconnaissance plane that simultaneously provided signals intelligence. The EA-6B (a four-seated variant of the A-6 Intruder) provided an electronic warfare (EW) capability to disrupt the enemy's in-flight communications. The E-2C was an early warning airborne platform that could detect enemy bandits (and other threats) from distances beyond the F-14's range of sight. "We were concerned about two scenarios where the Libyans might try to target these assets," said Muczynski. The first scenario postulated that these planes would make easy fodder for a MiG-25 at altitudes of 70,000-80,000 feet. The second scenario foresaw the planes being targeted at lower altitudes by Libyan Mig-23s. Come what may, the Navy ultimately accepted the fact that risking reconnaissance and EW planes to enemy fire was simply the "cost of business."

On the morning of August 18, 1981, the missile-fire exercise began as scheduled. Aboard the *Nimitz*, VF-41 flew alongside her sister squadron VF-84 "Jolly Rogers." About 100 miles east, the *Forrestal* hosted two F-4 Phantom squadrons: VF-74 "Be Devilers" and Marine Corps Squadron VFMA-115 "Silver Eagles." Fighters from the *Nimitz* were responsible for patrolling the western and southern sections of the area designated for the open-ocean missile shoot. Accordingly, VF-41 and VF-84 would fly three Combat Air Patrols (CAPs) over their assigned sectors. These CAPs were essentially roving security patrols wherein the F-14s would steer away any foreign aircraft attempting to enter the practice area. The *Forrestal*, meanwhile, maintained two CAPs to the east of the firing area.

The arrival and the intentions of US naval forces to the Gulf of Sidra had not been a secret. Indeed, these maneuvers had been announced through the normal channels defined by the International Hydrographic Organization (IHO) and the International Maritime Organization (IMO). Still, altercations between the US and Libya in the Gulf of Sidra were nothing new. In 1973, for example, Libyan jets had fired on a US Air Force C-130 conducting signals intelligence along the coast. More recently, in 1980, Libyan fighters had attacked an Air Force RC-135 reconnaissance plane. In both engagements, there had been no casualties on either side. Consequently, neither Libya nor the US took any further action.

Deeper into the Mediterranean, however, most engagements with Libyan aircraft passed without incident. In fact, this morning of August 18 would be Lieutenant Muczynski's first encounter with a Libyan bandit. That day, all three CAPs from the *Nimitz* were engaged by Libyan probes. From Muczynski's plane (call-signed: *Fast Eagle 107*), he intercepted a Libyan MiG-25 Foxbat at close range. "Half of the time, we would intercept them and they would let us join right to the wing," he said. "It was pretty surreal to be a couple feet from a MiG-25 that, up to now, had only been a picture in a book." Muczynski also marveled at the massive size of the Foxbat's engine. After escorting the wayward MiG to the edge of the training area, the Libyan pilot ignited his afterburner and sped away from *Fast Eagle 107*. During these intercept maneuvers, Muczynski's wingman would follow the Libyan aircraft from a mile behind, ready to engage the bandit if it attacked Muczynski during escort. Returning to the *Nimitz* that evening, Muczynski compared notes with his fellow aviators. They, too, had seen their share of Libyan aircraft throughout the day—MiG-23s, MiG-25s, Su-22s, and French-built Mirage F1 fighters. Trading stories about their close encounters, the American pilots agreed that the Mirage flyers seemed to be the most aggressive.

Still, the men of VF-41 were none too impressed by their Libyan counterparts.

"We had been briefed," Muczynski said, "that the Libyan pilots did not like to fly at night, and didn't care much for flying over the water." Thus, CAPs from the *Nimitz* would continue to launch in the pre-dawn hours, conduct aerial refuels via A-6 or A-7 aerotankers, and return to station at sunrise.

An F-14 from Squadron VF-84 likewise lands on the deck of the *Nimitz* on August 1, 1981. Nicknamed the "Jolly Rogers," VF-84 had been featured heavily in the 1980 film *The Final Countdown*. (US Navy)

On the second day of the exercise—August 19, 1981—Muczynski and his RIO, Lieutenant James Anderson (call sign: "Amos"), expected nothing more than a repeat of their first day. Early that morning, launching from Catapult 1 aboard the *Nimitz* was Commander Henry Kleeman (call sign: "Hank"), piloting *Fast Eagle 102*. A 1965 Annapolis graduate and a decorated Vietnam veteran, Kleeman had recently assumed command of VF-41 and was elated to be taking part in another Combat Air Patrol. Manning Kleeman's backseat was his trusted RIO, Lieutenant David Venlet (call sign: "DJ"). Following suit on Catapult 2 were Muczynski and Anderson, aboard *Fast Eagle 107*. Thus far, the American CAPs had intercepted forty Libyan bandits, but there had been no exchange of fire. In fact, these Libyan intercepts seemed to be following a similar pattern to the Tu-95 encounters—a photo opportunity punctuated by rude hand gestures.

This morning of August 19, however, would be different.

As Kleeman and Muczynski went aloft, the attending E-2 Hawkeye directed *Fast Eagle 107* to the southern edge of the patrol area. Muczynski acknowledged the order and began his CAP along the pre-determined flight path.

But suddenly, Muczynski realized that he had no wingman.

Confident that the E-2 would send another F-14 to his position, Muczynski waited until he was certain that the Hawkeye crew had forgotten about him. Keying the radio, Muczynski politely asked if anyone intended to join him on the southern CAP. He was surprised, however, when the E-2 directed Kleeman to fly southward and join *Fast Eagle 107* on patrol. "Even though we were both section leads," Muczynski recalled, "he [Kleeman] was the squadron commanding officer, so I naturally passed the lead to him and flew the wingman position for him." Neither crew, however, expected to see much action along the southern front. From their dinner conversations the night before, both crews learned that the southern CAP had been the most uneventful of the patrol sectors.

While flying their CAP on the morning of August 19, Kleeman and Muczynski decided to make an early call for an aerial refuel tanker. Because they had seen no action along the southern CAP—and did not anticipate making enemy contact—Kleeman and Muczynski reasoned that they could refuel early, and then rotate to the western sector where they would be more likely to encounter Libyan bandits. At first, it seemed that their hunch had been correct—"we started hearing some of the VF-84 guys out in the west engaging bogies"—but at 7:15 that morning, Kleeman's and Muczynski's collective fortunes changed for the better.

As the pair of F-14s vectored westward, two Libyan Su-22 fighters took off from Girdibayah Air Base. At first, it seemed that the Su-22s had scrambled to intercept the squadron's S-3A Viking—a plane known for its anti-submarine and anti-ship missions. Today, however, this S-3 had been sent aloft as part of the missile exercise, radar-targeting the ships and letting them practice defensive maneuvers against mock missile attacks.

As the S-3 continued to fly its holding pattern fifteen miles from the Libyan coast, the *Nimitz* alerted the plane of the approaching Su-22s and ordered the S-3 crew to fly north. The S-3 descended quickly—10,000 feet per minute—while vectoring northward to avoid the incoming Libyan fighters. At the same time, the F-14s were ordered to "turn and burn, expedite intercept."

While the Tomcats moved closer, the Su-22s turned their attention as well, and flew to the F-14s' elevation at 20,000 feet. *Fast Eagle 102* and *Fast Eagle 107* could see both Su-22s approaching via the AWG-9 radar. Kleeman and Muczynski thus flew into a "sidestep" position to gain lateral separation from the incoming Sukhois. This maneuver would place the Tomcats well in order to turn behind the Libyans and "merge" when the opposing formations met. If Kleeman, as the flight leader, had to engage the bogey, Muczynski could pull up from behind and provide covering fire. As the pair of F-14s flew closer to the incoming Su-22s, Muczynski's position relative to Kleeman's plane

Fast Eagle 102, the plane piloted by Commander Henry Kleeman, who shot down one of the offending Libyan Su-22s during the dogfight of August 19, 1981. (US Navy)

Fast Eagle 107 (foreground), the plane piloted by Lieutenant Lawrence Muczynski, credited with downing the other Su-22 during the engagement of August 19, 1981. (US Navy)

confused the Libyans' ground controllers. Indeed, because of the distance between the Tomcats and the ground control radars, the Libyans were detecting only *one* American aircraft—Kleeman's.

Thus, it came as a great surprise to the Libyan pilots when, from a distance of eight miles, they visually identified *two* F-14s. Still, neither Kleeman, Muczynski, nor their RIOs expected this engagement to devolve into a dogfight. Collectively, they expected this to be just another "close encounter"—perhaps with a photo opportunity and a good round of colorful hand gestures. Muczynski even told Anderson to get his camera ready.

Closing in at a rate of more than 1,000 knots, Muczynski's radar malfunctioned. "We didn't know it at the time," he recalled, "but the short-range function had died"—and this would be problematic if Muczynski had to engage the Libyans from stand-off distances. Still, Muczynski and Anderson pressed on with their flight pattern.

Suddenly, at 7:18 AM, the lead Libyan pilot radioed to his wingman: "I'm preparing to fire," followed quickly by: "I've fired!"

The Libyans had just engaged American aircraft.

At first, Muczynski thought that the Libyan pilot's wing had suddenly caught fire. However, it took less than a second to realize that he and Kleeman were under hostile fire. The lead Su-22 had fired an AA-2 Atoll short-range missile. The lead Sukhoi had been aiming for Kleeman, but because the Libyan pilot had fired his missile as a "hip-shoot," it missed *Fast Eagle 102* by a wide margin.

All told, these Su-22s had picked the wrong fight on the wrong day. For even at maximum armament, the Su-22 was little match for the F-14 Tomcat. Whether armed with R3-S or AA-2 missiles, the Sukhoi was still less maneuverable than the F-14, and its cockpit view was highly restrictive.

After the Libyan pilot had missed his intended target, both F-14s went on the attack. The Su-22s, perhaps in a state of panic, split their formation and the Tomcats turned to give chase. Muczynski descended from Kleeman's two o' clock position, giving chase to the lead Sukhoi. Kleeman radioed:

"Where are you going and what are you doing?"

"I've got the lead and the guy who shot at us," replied Muczynski.

"Roger," said Kleeman, "I've got the wingman."

Maneuvering *Fast Eagle 102* against the trailing bandit, Kleeman acquired missile lock for the AIM-9L Sidewinder. Unfortunately, he couldn't fire right away because both he and the bandit were facing the sun. It was a well-known fact among fighter pilots that one couldn't employ a heat-seeking missile while facing the sun, otherwise the missile would guide onto the sun instead of onto the intended target. Once clear of the sun, however, Kleeman depressed the trigger, firing his first Sidewinder in combat. *Fast Eagle 102* was approximately 40 degrees off the tail of the fleeing Sukhoi, at a distance of nearly one mile. The Libyan pilot, obviously sensing the missile lock, attempted an evasive maneuver but to no avail.

Indeed, the Sidewinder hit the Libyan bandit at a near-perfect 90-degree angle.

The force of impact sheared off the tail section and inadvertently deployed the drag chute—which the Su-22s used for their landings. The pilot ejected, deploying his own parachute and drifting down into the gulf below.

Meanwhile, *Fast Eagle 107* was hot on the trail of the lead Sukhoi. "I'm trying all kinds of things to get a radar lock," Muczynski recalled, "which was never going to happen," considering that his radar had died only moments ago. Finally, Muczynski pulled up the nose of his aircraft, preparing to fire his AIM-9 missile via boresight. Suddenly, from the backseat, Anderson cried out:

"Someone's been hit, someone's been shot!"

"Who is it?"

"I can't tell."

Frustrated, Muczynski looked off the port side of his aircraft to see a small black dot followed by a trail smoke descending towards the Gulf of Sidra. Hoping that this hurtling airframe hadn't been *Fast Eagle 102*, Muczynski called out to his commander:

"What should I do with this guy?!"

"Shoot! Shoot! SHOOT!" yelled Kleeman.

Having confirmed that his commander was still alive, Muczynski pulled the trigger and launched a Sidewinder missile straight into the tailpipe of the remaining Su-22. The resulting explosion was so close that Muczynski had to yank the Tomcat into a 10.2g climb to avoid the debris from the destroyed bandit. As he recalled: "We were inside half a mile when I shot, and now I'm closing in on all this debris at 500 knots, so I take both hands on the stick and pull for all I'm worth, because if there's one thing the Tomcat will do, it's pitch like a son-of-a-gun." All told, Muczynski didn't want debris from the exploding Sukhoi to fly through the canopy or into the Tomcat's air intake. The resulting 10.2g climb was such that both Anderson and Muczynski got the dreaded "tunnel vision," but luckily neither man blacked out.

Recovering from the climb, Muczynski called out to the *Nimitz*: "Fox 2 kill from Music"—indicating that he had downed the offending aircraft with a Sidewinder missile.

The entire engagement had lasted a mere 44 seconds.

From their vantage points, the F-14 crews noted that both Libyan pilots had ejected, but confirmed seeing only one parachute.

Taking pause to regain their bearings, Kleeman and Muczynski vectored north, returning to the *Nimitz*. As far as Kleeman and Muczynski were concerned, they were still in enemy territory and wanted to "bug out" before any more Libyan bandits came their way. As the adrenaline subsided, however, both F-14s fielded a flurry of radio inquiries from the *Nimitz* and the other CAPs. Apparently, the E-2 Hawkeye and the battle group commander thought Anderson had said "My leader's been shot!"—prompting the battle group to divert four additional Tomcats to the scene of the encounter. By the time these reinforcements arrived, however, Kleeman and Muczynski were preparing to leave the area. Thus, the now six F-14s took up formation and headed back to the flight deck.

Landing on the *Nimitz*, Kleeman, Venet, Muczynski, and Anderson were given a heroes' welcome. While *Fast Eagle 107* was getting "chained and chalked" on the flight deck, Muczynski shut down his portside engine and was preparing to shut down the starboard engine when the Master Caution Light suddenly illuminated. Curiously, Muczynski looked at his instrument panel to see that the "LADDER" light was activated—meaning that the boarding ladder was down. Looking back to the left, Muczynski was startled to see his plane captain (a junior maintenance technician) happily banging on the canopy. Wanting to dismount his Tomcat, Muczynski motioned for him to get down. But the young plane captain signaled for Muczynski to wait—producing a can of black spray paint and a stencil with the outline of a MiG. Muczynski marveled as the young technician sprayed a silhouetted MiG "kill" marking onto the F-14 before the plane had even shut down.

"He was that proud," said Muczynski.

Shutting down their aircraft, the crews of *Fast Eagle 102* and *Fast Eagle 107*, received a throng of handshakes and high-fives. Making their way through the crowded flight deck, the four heroes were soon met by the Admiral's aide.

"Guys, come with me," said the aide. It was time for debriefing.

Kleeman, Muczynski, Venet, and Anderson were given just enough time to change out of their flight gear before being shuffled up to the bridge. The commanding officer of the *Nimitz* was Captain Jack Batzler, and he wanted to hear the flight crews' rendition of the engagement. Kleeman did most of the talking and, after getting a picture of all four airmen, Batzler had the Admiral's aide take them below deck to the Intelligence personnel. "They separated us into four separate rooms with a pencil and paper," Muczynski recalled, "and told us each to write what we saw and what we did. I thought that was pretty amazing; they were making sure we were on the level, and there was no collusion." Later that day, the four men debriefed the Admiral who gave them hearty congratulations.

Several hours later, Muczynski was approached by one of the senior maintenance chiefs. The chief petty officer asked Muczynski if he had "over-G'd" the plane—meaning that he had taken the plane beyond its normal serviceability rating for gravitational forces in flight. Recalling his steep climb to avoid the debris from the Su-22, Muczynski sheepishly guessed that he had taken the F-14 to about 6.5g—a level that would certainly qualify for over-G'ing the plane. Typically, if a pilot over-G'd his plane, he would help the maintenance crew pull the aircraft's panels for inspection. Smiling, however, the maintenance chief leaned in and said: "Well, sir, it was 10.2g, and I'm going to give you

One of several press conferences involving the crews of *Fast Eagle 102* and *Fast Eagle 107*. The Gulf of Sidra Incident made headline news around the world, and Muczynski recalled receiving hundreds of congratulatory letters. With memories of Vietnam and the Iranian Revolution still fresh in America's collective memory, it seemed that many Americans were delighted by this aerial victory. As news of the incident spread, some American movie theaters posted on their marquees: "USN 2; Libya 0." (US Navy)

a free one for doing a hell of a job today."

Although the Gulf of Sidra Incident lasted less than a minute, the aftershocks were felt around the world. The United States finally saw what the F-14 could do in aerial combat. The US had shown the Gaddafi regime how quickly they would retaliate if provoked. Moreover, the Gulf of Sidra affair put the rest of the military world on notice—demonstrating how well the newest American fighters could maneuver against latter-day Soviet aircraft. Muczynski, Kleeman, Venet, and Anderson became national heroes. "We had multiple press conferences," Muczynski recalled, and the four men received congratulatory letters from around the world.

Later in the day on August 19, the US filed a complaint with the United Nations Security Council, arguing that the Libyan Air Force had attacked them unprovoked, during regular FON exercises in international airspace—exercises which had been announced through the proper channels on August 12 and 14.

Libya, of course, disagreed—filing a counter-response with the UN soon thereafter.

According to Libya, the US had provoked the altercation by deliberately flying into Libyan airspace. The conventions of international law, however, clearly favored the US position. Emerging from the UN, American emissaries reiterated that "any further attacks against US forces operating in international water and airspace will also be resisted with force if necessary."

In the years that followed, the US Navy continued its Freedom of Navigation exercises in the Mediterranean and elsewhere. However, its showdowns with the Gaddafi regime were far from over.

Upon completing his tour with Squadron VF-41, Larry Muczynski was assigned to the US Navy's Training Command, wherein he served as a flight instructor at Naval Air Station Meridian. He later served as a flight instructor at Naval Air Station Oceana, flying the F-14 Tomcat with Squadron VF-1486. Before his retirement in 1996, Muczynski commanded Squadron VF-201 "Hunters" at Naval Air Station Dallas. The assignment was fortuitous for Muczynski because VF-201 was in the midst of transitioning from F-4s to F-14s. By the time Muczynski left the service, he had logged more than 3,000 flight hours aboard the F-14. After leaving the Navy, Muczynski flew commercial airliners for the next several years.

Dave Venlet, Commander Kleeman's RIO, remained on active duty for the next 32 years. Shortly after the Gulf of Sidra, Venlet re-designated as a naval aviator—thus upgrading from RIO to pilot. As a newly-minted aviator, he flew F-14s with Squadron VF-143 "Pukin' Dogs" as an F-14 pilot embarked upon the USS *Eisenhower*. Venlet then served with Squadron VF-101 "Grim Reapers," at Naval Air Station Oceana as a Tomcat instructor pilot and an A-4 adversary pilot. Venlet would later go on to command the US Naval Air Systems Command and served as the executive officer of the F-35 Lightning II Program. He retired in 2013 at the rank of Vice Admiral.

Tragically, Henry "Hank" Kleeman died in a training accident four years after the Gulf of Sidra Incident. On December 3, 1985, Kleeman was the commanding officer of Test and Evaluation Squadron 4 (VX-4). That morning, he was piloting an F/A-18 Hornet from San Clemente Island en route to Naval Air Station Miramar (the famous "Fightertown USA"). At 8:48 AM, Kleeman radioed the tower at Miramar, advising them of his approach. The senior petty officer in the tower acknowledged the transmission:

"Roger, 620 [Kleeman's call sign] you are clear to continue. Duty runway is two-four [24]. Miramar is VFR [Visual Flight Rules; indicating fair weather and clear visibility]. There is standing water on the runway. Call the break, over."

Moments later, the tower petty officer identified Kleeman's and his wingman's planes—the pair of F/A-18s were on approach at nearly 300 knots descending from 4,000 feet. As Kleeman came within sight of Runway 24, he radioed: "Miramar Tower, this is 620 in the break, over."

"Roger, 620, take it around," replied the tower petty officer.

The petty officer, however, repeated his earlier warning of standing water on the runway. His radio transmission continued: "It will take a few minutes for crash vehicles to clear the runway. Call re-entering the break, over." Kleeman and his wingman acknowledged the transmission and entered a holding pattern, while the crash vehicles vacated the runway. The greater concern, however, was the standing water.

Fewer things present a danger to landing aircraft than water on the runway. Like automobiles, aircraft tires can also "hydroplane" when making contact with water at certain speeds. As a general rule: the greater the tire pressure, the greater the chance of hydroplaning. As Kleeman followed his wingman onto the runway, all seemed fine until his front wheel touched down. After rolling nearly 3,000 feet down the runway, Kleeman's F/A-18 suddenly began to hydroplane. Kleeman applied the brakes to no

A Tomcat from Squadron VF-84 stands proudly on the carrier deck. (US Navy)

avail. Having lost the vital friction needed for braking, the airplane drifted to the right and careened off the runway at a speed of 82 miles per hour. As the right side of the plane plowed into the ground, the force of impact flipped the F/A-18 upside down, wherein it skidded to a halt, separating the canopy from the fuselage.

Watching this horror unfold from the tower, the senior petty officer scrambled the evacuation crew, who then sped to the wreckage site. When the first crash truck arrived at 9:11 AM, the rescue squad found Kleeman unresponsive with this helmeted head jammed into the dirt. Although unresponsive, Kleeman still had a pulse and was thus still alive when the ambulance crew extracted him from the wreckage at 9:22. Meanwhile, the crash recovery crew worked frantically to keep the F/A-18 from exploding. Despite the impact of the crash (and being upside down) the plane's engines were still running. Being unable to reach the throttle and on-board avionics, the recovery crew simply extinguished the F/A-18's engine with water. Kleeman was pronounced dead at 10:31 that morning. The cause of death was determined to be a severed spinal cord, which Kleeman had broken upon the plane's inverted impact. He was 42 years old.

Likewise, James Anderson, Muczynski's RIO, met an untimely demise. Following his tour with Squadron VF-4, Anderson continued to serve in operational F-14 assignments. By 1989, he had risen to the rank of Lieutenant Commander and was happily assigned to Squadron VF-201 (the unit that, ironically, his former pilot Muczynski would later command). In March of that year, Anderson was on a much-needed vacation in Aspen, Colorado, enjoying his hand at Alpine skiing. On Saturday, March 11, 1989, Anderson was enjoying the slopes at a local ski resort when he crashed into a grove of trees. He was killed shortly upon impact. He was 37 years old.

Although two of the heroes from the Gulf of Sidra Incident have tragically passed on, the legacy of these naval airmen, and the reliability of the F-14 Tomcat, endures to this day. As Muczynski recalled: "This was the first time for the F-14 to prove itself in combat, and I think it was a big boost for the morale of the community, Grumman, and the country as a whole…and for the first time in a long time, Americans knew that the US would not take it lying down. You saw on theater marques, 'USN-2; Libya-0' and all kinds of things. But we just did what we were trained to do, and all the training and equipment worked as advertised." Muczynski was quick to point out that any of his squadron mates could have done what he, Anderson, Kleeman, and Venet had done. "We just happened to be there at the right time, in the right place, with the right results."

Tomcats over Iran

Throughout the Tomcat's illustrious history, the Islamic Republic of Iran has been its only foreign operator. By 1970, the US had no closer ally in the Middle East than Iran. Known internationally as "Persia" until 1935, the Imperial State of Iran was the dominion of the Pahlavi dynasty—the latest ruling family in what had been 2,000 years of monarchial rule. Mohammed Reza Pahlavi, officially known as the

The inaugural group of Tomcat pilots for the Imperial Iranian Air Force pose for a group photo at the Khatami Air Base, 1975. (IIAF)

"Shah of Iran," had ruled his kingdom as somewhat of an absolute monarch following his assumption to the throne in 1941. Maintaining close ties to the US, the Shah employed several thousand American workers in support of Iran's oil industry. The Shah's interest in the F-14 Tomcat, however, began amidst the political dealings of his chief rivals—the Soviet Union and the Republic of Iraq.

On April 9, 1972—as part of the Iraqi-Soviet Treaty of Friendship and Cooperation—the Soviet Ministry of Defense approved the sale of several new fighter aircraft to the Iraqi Air Force—including the vaunted MiG-25 "Foxbat." Not wanting to be outclassed by his Arab rival (or slighted by the Soviet menace) Mohammed Reza Pahlavi solicited a meeting with US envoys to discuss the purchase of new weaponry. Having been a pilot himself, the Shah was particularly interested in acquiring a new fighter jet.

In May of that year, President Richard Nixon and National Security Advisor Henry Kissinger traveled to meet with Pahlavi in Tehran. Prior to that meeting, however, Kissinger advised Nixon to be judicious when offering weapons to the Shah. Accordingly, Kissinger recommended offering just the F-4 Phantom and F-5 Tiger—both in limited quantities. He further recommended leaving the new F-14 Tomcat and F-15 Eagle out of the negotiations. Although Kissinger wanted to maintain strong ties with Iran, he nevertheless believed that the best equipment should be reserved for American personnel. In the meeting with Pahlavi, however, Nixon ignored Kissinger's advice and offered the Shah access to purchase nearly anything he wanted—including the F-14, F-15, and the burgeoning arsenal of laser-guided munitions. The US State Department later referred to Nixon's offer as a "blank check" that allowed Iran to purchase everything "short of the atomic bomb."

Although bristled by Nixon's generosity towards the Shah, Henry Kissinger nevertheless defended his president's actions. In a later message, Kissinger stated that the President's commitment to the Shah aligned with the policy "to encourage purchase of US equipment" and that the acquisition process "should be left in the hands of the Iranian Government" without "restrictions other than the normal licensing and legal requirements" placed on US firms involved in the transaction.

This agreement between President Nixon and the Shah of Iran paved the way for a sizeable delivery of American military equipment. Indeed, from 1972-76, the Imperial State of Iran became the largest single buyer of American weaponry, spending more than $10 billion. Central to the Nixon-Pahlavi agreement, however, was the F-14 Tomcat.

The Imperial Iranian Air Force (IIAF) would ultimately order 80 Tomcats from Grumman Aerospace. On January 7, 1974, US and Iranian representatives signed the contract for Project Persian King—the official codename for the $300 million program delivering 30 F-14A jets along with spare parts, replacement engines, and a full complement of munitions, including more than 400 AIM-54 Phoenix missiles. That June, the IIAF ordered an additional 50 F-14As along with another 290 Phoenix missiles.

For the Iranian Ministry of Defense, and the pilots of the IIAF, the F-14 presented a great opportunity. According to Captain Rassi, one of Iran's inaugural Tomcat pilots, the IIAF had been longing for a fighter that was "superior in maneuverability and weaponry" while simultaneously providing "a highly-flexible area defense interceptor." Several Iranian pilots had test-flown the F-15 Eagle during the early days of their fighter acquisition process, but none were impressed by its handling or its performance. "The

An early Iranian Tomcat takes flight, 1976. (IIAF)

F-15A was pleasant to fly due to its flight control augmentation system, which was a major improvement at the time."

But, as Rassi noted, the Tomcat outperformed the Eagle in lower-altitude engagements.

"With pilots of equal skill," he recalled, "the F-14A always wins against the F-15A." Indeed, Rassi had piloted the F-15 in mock dogfights against American F-14s—and he was defeated every time. "We wanted a complete system," he continued, "including superior sensors, effective long-range weapons and man-machine interface that would need little or no outside support. We simply couldn't ignore the F-14. Its performance during the war with Iraq confirmed our decision beyond any doubt."

Delivery of the Iranian F-14s began in January 1976, flown to Iran by US Navy pilots from the Grumman facility in Calverton, New York. Aside from their distinctive camouflage scheme, the Iranian F-14s were practically identical to their US Navy counterparts. Both possessed the AWG-9 radar and carried the AIM-54 Phoenix missiles. Granted, the

Jalil Zandi, pictured here in 1977, was the most-decorated F-14 pilot in Iranian history. Following the Islamic Revolution, Zandi was labeled one of the "Shah's pilots" and was sentenced to ten years imprisonment. However, when the Iran-Iraq War began in 1980, he was released from prison due to his expertise in piloting the F-14. In combat, he scored 11 aerial victories—shooting down Iraqi MiG-21s, MiG-23s, and Mirage F1s. Zandi was tragically killed in an automobile accident in April 2001. (IIAF)

AWG-9's radar frequency was slower aboard the Iranian exports, but only by 1/100th of a second. The Iranian version also did not possess the AN/ALR-23 IRST (Infrared Scanner/Tracker), nor did it have the AN/ARA-62 instrument landing system for carrier recoveries. This exported version also carried AIM-54 missiles with downgraded electronic countermeasure suites to make them less effective in combat against US-built aircraft. Nevertheless, the Imperial State of Iran now possessed the most technologically-advanced fighter jet in the Western arsenal. All they needed now were trained pilots.

For its inaugural training program, the IIAF established a hub for Tomcat operations near the city of Isfahan, in central Iran. Known as Tactical Fighter Base 8, the aerodrome was later nicknamed "Khatami," after the legendary IIAF Commander-in-Chief, General Mohammed Amir Khatami. The late Commander-in-Chief had been killed in a glider accident on September 12, 1975. Prior to his untimely death, he had been the chief air advisor to the Shah, and was the Shah's brother-in-law.

To assist with the operations at Khatami Air Base, both Grumman and the US Navy sent a team of pilots to establish a training curriculum. Almost simultaneously, the IIAF sent a handful of its best fighter pilots to Naval Air Station Miramar for F-14 familiarization. Taking lessons from Squadron VF-124 "Gunfighters," this group of Iranian pilots would become the first F-14 instructors in the IIAF.

Bearing the new insignia of the Islamic Republic of Iran Air Force (IRIAF), this F-14 prepares to land at Mehrabad. (Shahram Sharifi)

Alongside these Iranian F-14 instructors, the US Navy graciously provided 27 pilot-instructors to Khatami Air Base from 1976-79. During this time, hundreds of Iranian groundcrews and pilots received their training and qualifications. The IIAF was proud of its investment; and the pilots clearly valued their newfound airframe. As former Iranian pilot, Captain Javad recalled:

"I found the F-14A light years ahead right from the start of my training. I had no problems in leaving my F-4 Phantom II squadron for a new Tomcat unit. I loved the Phantom II, but learned to love the F-14A even more. Every pilot falls in love with an aircraft or two during his career, but there will always be one favorite, and mine was without a doubt the desert-camouflaged F-14. When I touched it for the first time I was overcome with pride, and I felt honored to be a part of the program."

While climbing aboard this Tomcat for its maiden flight, Javad was suddenly stopped by the IIAF commander...and Shah Mohammed Reza Pahlavi himself. "His Majesty saw me and three other pilots admiring our new aircraft," said Javad. The Shah approached Javad and his comrades and, after exchanging salutes, asked Javad what he thought of the IIAF's newest fighter. Javad replied:

"I couldn't think of a better fighter in the world to defend Iran than the F-14 Tomcat."

Shah Pahlavi smiled and replied, "Captain, there is no better fighter in the world, and that is exactly why we have them in our air force. However, Captain, I must give you an order that will challenge you and place a great burden on your shoulders, and the shoulders of your colleagues—master the Tomcat and its weapons systems without delay. The F-14, and its advanced systems, will never be better than the pilots we trust to fly

The Ayatollah Ali Khamenei inspects an F-14 at the Shahid Babaie Air Base, 1990. In the wake of the Islamic Revolution, the new government briefly considered selling the Tomcats back to the United States. However, the Iranians soon realized that the F-14 was too powerful an asset to discard. (IRIAF)

them in defense of our nation. So, you, Captain, must always strive to be the best."

During the twilight of his reign, the Shah was so impressed by the F-14, that he solicited President Jimmy Carter for an additional seventy planes. Ultimately, the Shah wanted to spend another $2 billion to expand the IIAF. Unfortunately, Pahlavi would never fulfill his ambitions for the Persian military. Indeed, by 1978, the Shah's power had begun collapsing under the fury of the Islamic Revolution. Although Iran had been slowly rising as a modern-day, secularized economic power, years of heavy-handed rule under the House of Pahlavi had taken its toll on the Iranian people. Spearheaded by the Ayatollah Khomeini, the Revolution promised an end to the Shah's rule, and a restoration of Persian glory by way of an Islamic theocracy. As the mass protests paralyzed Iran from within, the Shah abdicated his throne on January 16, 1979. Following the Shah's departure and his subsequent exile, the Ayatollah Khomeini and his acolytes established the radical theocracy that they had promised. With the stroke of a pen, the Imperial State of Iran had become the Islamic Republic of Iran. Throughout the following year, Mohammed Reza Pahlavi drifted from one country to another—officially a "guest of the state" looking for permanent sanctuary. By this time, however, the Shah had been suffering from a long bout of cancer, which ultimately took his life on July 27, 1980.

The new Islamic regime, however, had a tremendous impact on the Iranian F-14 program. As the Revolutionary government purged itself of all things Pahlavi, the Ayatollah began targeting military officers who had been loyal to the Shah. Twenty-seven of Iran's best Tomcat pilots fled the country. Many of the original F-14 trainees were derided as being the "Shah's Pilots" and were either imprisoned, harassed, or kept under heavy surveillance.

The Islamic Revolution had also disrupted Iran's relationship with the United States. When the members of the Revolution took hostages at the American Embassy in Tehran, the US severed diplomatic relations with the new Iranian government. All US Navy instructors and technicians were recalled from their posts, leaving behind only eighty Iranian technicians for a fleet of seventy-seven F-14s.

As the Islamic Republic of Iran chartered its new government, most of its F-14s were temporarily grounded. At one point, the new government had even considered selling them back to the United States. In the end, however, Iran decided to keep its fleet of F-14s—incorporating them into the new Islamic Republic of Iran Air Force (IRIAF). Although the anti-Western, Islamic purists resented having these new-fangled American jets, they nevertheless realized that the F-14 was too much of an equalizer to discard. Likewise, for the burgeoning Islamic government, the F-14 provided a wonderful asset to an expanding military force.

Coincidentally, in the wake of Iran's decision to retain the F-14, the plane would prove its worth in combat against the Iraqi Air Force.

Although technically allies, the Iranians and Iraqis had never fully trusted one another. Border disputes between the two nations had been ongoing for years. And since the assassination of Egyptian President Gamal Nasser in 1970, both Iraq and Iran had been jockeying to become the dominant force in the Middle East. After the downfall of the Shah, however, Saddam Hussein, the president of Iraq, took warning of the Ayatollah's rhetoric. Saddam, and many within his Ba'ath Party government, were Sunni Muslims.

The majority of Iraq's citizens, however, were Shiite Muslims—just like the Ayatollah and his disciples. Fearing that the Ayatollah's rhetoric would galvanize Iraq's Shiite majority, the "Butcher of Baghdad" launched a preemptive invasion of Iran on September 22, 1980. Simultaneously, Saddam had hoped to take advantage of the instability following the Shah's exile, and seize key petroleum fields along the Iranian border. For the next eight years, the ensuing Iran-Iraq War would cost thousands of lives and ended in a bloody stalemate.

During the opening volleys of the conflict, however, the IRIAF scrambled every available F-14, taking flight to intercept the Iraqi MiGs. Even before the official start of the war, Iranian F-14s had intercepted a number of Iraqi air patrols. For example, on September 7, 1980, five Iraqi Mi-25 "Hind" helicopters ventured into Iranian airspace in the Zain al-Qaws region, attacking Iranian Army outposts along the border.

Two F-14s scrambled to intercept.

After a few minutes aloft, the lead Tomcat acquired the Iraqi helicopters on his radar, and descended to engage. Determined to destroy these offending aircraft before they returned to Iraqi airspace, the lead F-14 acquired his first missile lock with an AIM-9 Sidewinder. Firing the first missile, it quickly lost its lock-on (possibly disrupted by the heat of the ground) and plummeted into the desert, landing behind the trailing helicopter. Undeterred, the Iranian pilot fired a second Sidewinder which, again, failed to acquire its target and speared into the ground. By this time, however, the pilot had closed within range to engage the helicopters with his Vulcan gun. As the pilot depressed the trigger, the Vulcan expelled a deadly 400-round burst, splashing the trail helicopter, and sending its fiery carcass hurtling into the desert floor.

It was the first aerial kill in history for the F-14 Tomcat.

This skirmish over the Iranian borderlands would be the first of many victories for the IRIAF during the war.

A few more skirmishes followed during the weeks prior to September 22. One such engagement, occurring on September 13, saw the first MiG-23 shot down by an Iranian F-14. Major Mohammed-Reza Attaie, assigned to the 81st Tactical Fighter Squadron at Khatami Air Base, went aloft that day carrying the AIM-54 Phoenix missile, which the IRIAF had recently approved for combat use during border patrols. After spending considerable time with no activity along his patrol front, Attaie finally spotted the Iraqi MiG-23 and skillfully downed the bandit with a missile shot.

In the days prior to the invasion, more Iranian F-14s were brought back into operational status. Concurrently, many of the blacklisted pro-Shah Tomcat pilots were released from prison, though many were scrutinized for years afterward. Despite the revitalization of its F-14 fleet, however, no Tomcats were in the sky on the morning of September 22. Indeed, it was not until the following day that Iran's F-14s went airborne - escorting a flight of KC707s to the Iraqi border in support of the F-4 Phantom strike missions.

While flying border patrol missions, these Iranian Tomcats participated in numerous dogfights against the Iraqi MiGs and Sukhois. The geopolitical irony of this air combat was apparent: indeed, the much-anticipated showdown between American and Soviet-built aircraft was playing out not in the skies over Europe, but in the Persian Gulf. On September 24, in a single day of combat, Iranian F-14s claimed half a dozen kills—including MiG-21s, MiG23s, and Su-22s. The following day, a pair of Tomcats scrambled

Two Iranian Tomcats take flight armed with a complement of AIM-7, AIM-9, and AIM-54 missiles. The F-14 on the left appears to be carrying an additional MIM-23 Hawk missile. As the Iran-Iraq War continued, the number of combat-capable F-14s diminished. Having severed ties with the United States, the Iranian military no longer had access to spare parts or technical expertise needed to maintain their fleet of Tomcats. (IRIAF)

into Iraqi airspace to help evacuate two battle-damaged F-4 Phantoms. Coming to the aid of their beleaguered comrades, these F-14s helped the Phantoms escape from Iraqi airspace, simultaneously downing a MiG-21 and two MiG-23s near Baghdad. The pace of these air-to-air victories continued and, by November 1980, Iranian F-14s had confirmed at least 25 kills.

As Captain Javad, the Iranian pilot who extolled the Tomcat's virtues to the Shah, recalled: "It was clear to any Iranian pilot who flew over the frontlines that there was a war going on." During those first two months of the war, the IRIAF and its Tomcats set the tempo and retained the initiative for the remainder of the air campaign. Iran's Army, however, still reeling from the aftershocks of the Revolution, was slower in stemming the tide of Iraqi aggression. In the air, however, the IRIAF dominated the Iraqi Air Force almost from the outset. "There was little on the ground to stop the massed Iraqi Army from rolling east," Javad continued. "Our air force," on the other hand, "intercepted Iraqi fighters over the border, bombed the Iraqis on the ground, and launched air strikes deep into enemy airspace."

The only liability to the Tomcats' performance was their perennial shortage of ground crew support. Indeed, every mission created the possibility for more mechanical failures and/or battle damage that couldn't be fixed. Following the exodus of Grumman and US Navy personnel from Iran (and the severance of diplomatic ties to the United States), Iran

Five Iranian F-14s in formation. At the beginning of the Iran-Iraq War, the IRIAF had 80 combat-capable F-14s. By 1988, that number had fallen to less than 25. Today, barely a dozen Tomcats remain operational. (Shahram Sharifi)

faced economic sanctions preventing them from receiving any spare parts or ammunition for the F-14. Thus, if a critical component aboard the F-14 broke, the IRIAF would not have the requisite spare parts, or even the mechanical expertise needed to fix it.

Thus, the lack of spare parts and technical knowledge hamstrung the Iranian F-14s as the war dragged on. As one pilot recalled, "The Tomcat was a good dogfighter and a formidable challenge to any Iraqi MiG or Mirage. But our F-14s had problems as well. The dwindling number of flyable airframes and never-ending engine problems kept us from becoming true hunter-killers and destroying everything that came our way." By 1984, it was reported that the IRIAF had only 40 operational Tomcats.

By 1986, that number had fallen to 25.

One year later, less than half of the airworthy Tomcats still had working radars. Ironically, as parts and ammunition grew scarce, the IRIAF had to rely on third-party (i.e. black market) arms dealers to fill the shortages. Still, the number of battle-ready Tomcats continued to decline.

Despite these limitations, however, Iranian pilots genuinely admired the F-14. In combat against the MiG-23, MiG-25, and French-built Mirage F1, Iranian pilots always felt they had the upper hand. According to Major Farhad Nassirkhani, "The capability of the F-14A to snap around during the dogfight was unequalled.... After only 100 hours of training, I learned to pitch the nose of my Tomcat up at a 75-degree [angle of attack] in just over a second, turn around, and acquire the opponent either with Sidewinders or the gun."

The Iraqi Air Force was equally impressed by the Tomcat.

Aside from the F-14's superior maneuverability, Iraqi pilots marveled at (and were simultaneously frightened by) the AWG-9 radar. Of the F-14's avionics, the AWG-9 was perhaps the most reliable. In many respects, it enabled the Tomcat pilots to see and shoot father than their MiG-based counterparts. Years later, another Iranian pilot remarked: "During the whole war, I never heard of the AWG-9 radar being successfully jammed. There were a handful of cases of radar lock-on being broken by close-range maneuvering or by MiG-25s using their high speed to outrun an F-14 but the Iraqis and Soviets never managed to jam our radars."

Capitalizing on the Iraqis' fear of the F-14, and tempering it against the lack of available technical support, the IRIAF used the Tomcat primarily as a deterrent. Accordingly, the Iranians would send the F-14 into designated "hot spots" to provide a presence that few Iraqi aircraft wanted to challenge. As Major Nassirkhani remarked: "The Iraqi high command had ordered all its pilots not to engage the F-14 and not get close if [an] F-14 is known to be operating in the area. Usually the presence of Tomcats was enough to scare the enemy and send the Iraqi fighters back."

Meanwhile, Captain Hashemi, another F-14 pilot, noted that: "The MiG-23 was not the fighter the Iraqis had hoped for. It could not outmaneuver any of our fighters and we have had very little respect for them on a one-to-one basis. We were concerned only when facing large numbers of Iraqi MiG-23s, later during the war." Of the enemy planes that the Iranians met in the air, the MiG-23 seemed to be the most derided. Like the Tomcat, the MiG-23 featured the variable swept-wing design, but its mechanical clumsiness made the swing wing a liability during air-to-air combat. As Major Ali, another F-14 pilot, recalled: "The MiG-23 was nowhere near an equal opponent for us. It had good acceleration, which made it easy for the Iraqis to escape, but still they suffered constant losses."

Despite the obvious intimidation factor, several Iraqi pilots nevertheless tested their mettle against the F-14.

None of these attempts ended well for the Iraqi airmen.

For instance, on December 1, 1980, Iranian F-14s from the 82d Tactical Fighter Squadron destroyed three Iraqi fighters in a single engagement. The following day, a lone Tomcat from the 82d scored an impressive aerial victory while outnumbered 4-to-1. Piloted by Captain F. Dehghan and his RIO, this lone Tomcat had been flying a combat air patrol covering Khark Island as well as the Cyrus and Nowrouz oil rigs. After several monotonous orbits around his patrol region, however, Dehghan was intercepted by two Iraqi MiG-21s and two Su-20s. Undeterred by the odds, Dehghan maneuvered to engage the bandits, closing within ten miles, while the RIO chose to attack with "Pulse Single Target Track" mode, locking on to the lead MiG. Moments later, Dehghan fired a short-range AIM-54A Phoenix missile, destroying the lead bandit with a primitive fury. As the remaining bandits watched their comrade hurtling into the Persian Gulf, the Iraqi pilots wisely disengaged and fled to the north.

Encounters such as these occurred regularly over the next four years, as the Iraqi Air Force sent their normal variety of MiG-23s, MiG-25s, Su-20s, and Mirage F1s to probe the Iranian border and other strategic locations like Khark Island.

Time and again, Iranian F-14s were up to the task.

By 1984, these Tomcats had confirmed at least a dozen additional kills. As Captain

Javad explained, "The F-14 had become so feared by the IrAF [Iraqi Air Force] by then that when they were not airborne over Iran, Iraqi MiGs and Sukhois filled the sky like the 'birds of the Howr al-Howeizeh,' bombing our positions with ease. If there was no Tomcat over Khark or Tehran, the Iraqis would immediately attempt to strike. And it worked the other way around too—wherever IRIAF F-14s showed up, the Iraqis ran away."

Maintenance and serviceability issues aside, it seemed that bigger issue for Iran was the increasing hostility from the international community. The Ayatollah's firebrand rhetoric had not won him any friends in the West, and international opinion had begun to sway in favor of Iraq. As the war progressed, several leaders in the international community began to see Saddam Hussein as the lesser of two evils. Although he was a demonstrable despot, and clearly the aggressor in the Iran-Iraq War, Saddam would soon be characterized as a pro-Western, secular foil against the anti-Western, Islamic fundamentalists in Iran.

At the beginning of the Iran-Iraq War, the United States had declared neutrality. At first, the US regarded the Iran-Iraq affair as just another petty conflict in the Middle East. Although America's relationship with Iran had soured, the US had no fondness for Saddam Hussein. However, now that America and Iraq shared a common enemy in the Ayatollah, the US began providing technical support to the Iraqi war effort.

But as the Iran-Iraq War waxed and waned, so too did Iran's use of the F-14. By 1987, Tomcats were still intercepting Iraqi MiGs and Sukhois—confirming more aerial kills along the way—but the dwindling number of airworthy F-14s was hard to deny. Meanwhile, as part of its assistance to Iraq, the US Navy began patrolling the Persian Gulf, alerting Iraqi pilots of Iranian jets operating in the area. Thus, when Iranian F-14s arrived to intercept the Iraqis fighters, the enemy bandits had already eluded them.

By November 1987, the IRIAF had only fifteen Tomcats that were fully mission-capable. To make matters worse, they were running dangerously low on ammunition— fewer than fifty Phoenix missiles remained. Despite this, the IRIAF remained active during the latter years of the war, mostly in response to Iraq's increased vigor in the air. Bolstered by the arrival of the F1EQ Mirage fighter, as well as support from the United States and Saudi Arabia, Iraq went on the offensive.

Although Iran was now forced to defend itself against a better-armed and better-assisted enemy, they nevertheless held Iraqi forces at bay—on the ground and in the air. However, the new and improved F1EQ Mirage (supplied by France) was the biggest challenge that the Iranian F-14s had yet faced. With an improved radar and missile system, the F1EQ was a specially-built export version of the F1E, sold exclusively to Iraq. Although a formidable foe, Iranian F-14s still managed to hold their own against the new challenger.

One such engagement occurred on February 9, 1988.

As expected, the Iraqi Air Force was once again targeting Khark Island, and two Iranian F-14s were dispatched to defend it. Upon their arrival, the two Tomcats identified six enemy Mirages. The lead F-14, piloted by First Lieutenant Qiyassi, fired his first Sparrow missile from a distance of five and a half miles. Scoring a direct hit on one of the offending Mirages, he descended to a lower altitude in a defensive maneuver to avoid the other Mirages closing from either side. After leveling out his Tomcat, Qiyassi turned hard

An Iranian Tomcat pilot and his RIO prepare for a flight near Isfahan. As the number of airworthy Tomcats continued to diminish, the Iranian government began acquiring spare parts via third-party arms dealers. These backdoor supply networks later evaporated when the US destroyed its remaining F-14s and removed them from the surplus sales market. (Tasmin News Agency)

right, giving chase to another Mirage. Locking on to the fleeing fighter, he fired an AIM-9P, scoring a direct hit from the rear and sending the Mirage into a spectacular fireball.

Returning to Bushehr Air Base to refuel, Qiyassi was back in the air an hour later. Responding to an alert of incoming Iraqi aircraft, Qiyassi and his RIO ascended to 20,000 feet. Making several sweeps with their AWG-9 radar, however, neither crewman detected any enemy aircraft. Vectoring his plane to the southeast, Qiyassi was prepared to return to base when his RIO detected two bandits at a range of ten miles. As the F-14 jetted towards the marauding bandits, Qiyassi confirmed both aircraft as F1 Mirages.

Upon spotting the lone F-14, however, both F1s scattered and made a desperate dash towards Iraqi airspace. Trying to shake off their pursuer, the pair of Mirages descended quickly, taking high speeds at lower altitudes. Qiyassi, however, stayed right on their heels, settling in behind the lead Mirage. At 12:42 PM, Qiyassi fired his AIM-9P Sidewinder missile at the lead bandit, but noticed that the second Mirage was closing in on his tail. He was forced to break away and, hence, unable to confirm if his missile had destroyed the lead Mirage. Running his Tomcat fast and making multiple maneuvers to clear himself of the second Mirage, Qiyassi returned the spot where he had fired his Sidewinder. Scanning the air and the sea below, he was pleased to find the burning wreckage of the Mirage on the surface of the water. Qiyassi's kill was later confirmed by a group of sailors in a nearby convoy.

A few days later, on February 15, the Iraqi Air Force sent another sortie of Mirages against the oil terminal on Sirri Island. Although the pair of F1s were successful in their

This F-14, one of the few remaining airworthy Tomcats in Iran, stands on display at an IRIAF exhibition in 2016. (Tasmin News Agency)

bombing (and their attack had been covered by nearby US Navy ships), the Iraqi pilots were nonetheless caught off guard by the sudden appearance of an F-14 from the 81st Tactical Fighter Squadron. While the Mirages struggled to get their bearings, the lone F-14 calmly fired one of its Phoenix missiles, downing the lead bandit while the shell-shocked wingman bolted back towards Iraqi airspace.

The following day, another Tomcat, piloted by Major A. Rahnavard, went aloft from Bushehr Air Base. Despite being labeled a "Shah's Pilot," Rahnavard had somehow survived the post-Pahlavi purge. A distinguished aviator, Rahnavard had flown F-4s, F-5s, F-14s, and C-130 cargo planes in the Imperial Iranian Air Force. Perhaps buoyed by his flight experience and technical competence, Rahnavard was allowed to continue his service although, since 1979, he had been relegated to RIO positions. However, as the war dragged on, and the need for pilots increased, Rahnavard was restored to full pilot status. Although he never achieved the "ace" distinction (five confirmed kills), he was nevertheless considered a "Top Gun" in Iran.

On the morning of February 16, 1988, Rahnavard was flying a solo Combat Air Patrol near Khark Island when his RIO detected two flights of four incoming Iraqi fighters. Assessing their formation, Rahnavard realized they were employing the standard Iraqi tactic of overwhelming IRAIF Tomcats with a multi-directional attack. Rahnavard fired a Sparrow missile into the formation, hoping to disrupt their attack, but the AIM-7 malfunctioned and plummeted into the Persian Gulf.

Fearful that his remaining Sparrows would likewise malfunction, Rahnavard selected his Sidewinder missile. Climbing high, he dove out from under the sun and acquired missile lock on the first of the Mirage bandits. Firing his AIM-9 Sidewinder, Rahnavard vectored away as the missile turned the Mirage into a blazing fireball. Despite losing their comrade to an AIM-9, the Iraqi pilots had nevertheless succeeded in drawing the F-14 away from the incoming strike force. Indeed, while Rahnavard was engaging the first formation of Mirages, the latter formation had slipped through Iranian airspace and delivered their bombs on Khark Island.

Realizing there was little he could do to affect the Khark Island strike force, Rahnavard decided to disengage the current formation of Mirages and fly north to refuel from an airborne KC707. He still had three functional Sidewinders and wanted to use them against the other Mirages as they returned from their Khark Island bombing run.

Meanwhile, the Mirages over Khark Island had successfully completed their mission—despite losing their flight leader to a MIM-23 surface-to-air missile. While beginning their return flight to Iraq, however, the offending Mirages were intercepted by Rahnavard's F-14. Getting a lock onto the closest F1, Rahnavard fired another AIM-9 missile. At first, his heart sank as the missile appeared to lose its tracking and began vectoring towards the sea. But Rahnavard's disappointment quickly turned to bliss as the missile re-acquired its targets and slammed into the rear of the fleeting F1, sending its fiery fuselage hurtling into the waters below.

Engagements like Qiyassi's and Rahnavard's continued until July 1988. As one pilot recalled, it became "a sort of mini-war" between Tomcats and Mirages. Although the Tomcat was the undisputed victor, the F-14 pilots nevertheless admired the F1 Mirage as the best fighter they had yet encountered. However, the Tomcat's victory in this "mini-war" took Western observers by surprise. Indeed, by this time, few believed that the Iranian F-14s were still operational. Furthermore, none had expected the Iranian pilots to possess the degree of acumen that they had displayed in the dogfights against Iraqi Mirages.

Although these latter-day victories were impressive, by 1988 both sides were eager to end the conflict. True to form, the United Nation brokered a ceasefire agreement and subsequently negotiated a peace settlement between the warring parties. Under the banner of UN Resolution 598, Khomeini accepted the terms of the ceasefire.

The Iran-Iraq War thus ended on August 20, 1988.

Although both sides claimed victory, the Iranians and Iraqis had essentially fought each other to a draw. Saddam had failed to annex the Iranian territories he desired, and Khomeini had failed to topple Iraq's regime or decisively defeat its military. Post-bellum analyses aside, however, there can be little argument that the F-14 had proven its worth in sustained air-to-air combat.

After the war, the IRIAF conducted a full accounting of its aerial victories against the Iraqi Air Force. The exact numbers remain elusive, however, as both the Iraqis and Iranians had inflated their kill ratios for domestic propaganda. According to one postwar conference, the IRIAF achieved only 30 air-to-air victories (including 16 kills via the AIM-54 Phoenix missile). However, these numbers seem alarmingly low to the pilots who were directly involved in the air campaign. By their own estimate, the number of confirmed kills by IRIAF was closer to 130, with an additional 23 "probable" kills. In a similar vein, the final number of Tomcats lost to enemy fire remains unknown—

ranging from three to several dozen. Seven F–14s, however, were confirmed lost during operational or training accidents.

Today, Iran is the only country that still flies the F–14. As the US Navy retired its fleet of F–14s in 2006, the few dozen Tomcats in Iran are the only ones in the world that are still airworthy. Their maintenance and supply issues, however, remain unchanged. Indeed, the IRIAF perennially subsists on less than half the ammunition and spare parts needed to maintain a combat-capable fleet. Although the Iranian government had been able to acquire spare parts via the black market (that is, arms dealers who had purchased from US military surplus sales) these backdoor venues later evaporated as the Pentagon sponsored a $900,000 demolition program to destroy its remaining F–14s.

Although these Iranian Tomcats may not be operational beyond the year 2030, the F–14 has nevertheless achieved a noteworthy place in the history of Iran. More than forty years after its introduction to the Shah, the F–14 Tomcat remains the most celebrated fighter jet of the IRIAF.

Contingency Operations of the 1980s

Afer distinguishing itself in combat against Libyan Sukhois, the F-14 Tomcat's reputation continued to grow throughout the various contingency operations of the 1980s. As the United States ventured into smaller skirmishes around the world, the Tomcat remained at the forefront of America's military presence. During these

An F-14 Tomcat from Squadron VF-32 prepares to take flight off the coast of Lebanon, 1983. As part of the peacekeeping operation during the Lebanese Civil War, American F-14s flew aerial reconnaissance missions, utilizing their Tactical Airborne Reconnaissance Pod Systems (TARPS). (US Navy)

Aboard the USS *John C. Stennis,* a support crew prepares to affix the Tactical Airborne Reconnaissance Pod System (TARPS) to the fuselage of an F-14. The TARPS was a sophisticated camera system that could take high-resolution photographs on a variety of settings. American F-14s made extensive use of their TARPS in the skies over Lebanon and Grenada (US Navy)

engagements, the missions for the F-14 were as varied as the locations themselves. From notable actions such as the Lebanese Civil War, Operation Urgent Fury in Grenada, Operation El Dorado Canyon in Libya, the *Achille Lauro* incident, and the so-called "Tanker War" involving Iran and Iraq, the F-14 saw its reputation rise as one of the world's premier fighter jets.

Lebanese Civil War

In 1975, following years of sectarian tension, the state of Lebanon erupted into a civil war. This Lebanese Civil War, however, soon became a regional conflict—involving Maronite Christians, the Palestine Liberation Organization (PLO), Israel, and Syria. The fighting amongst the various combatants fluctuated in its severity until 1981, when the US brokered a ceasefire between Israel and the PLO to prevent the former's invasion of Lebanon.

This ceasefire, however, was short-lived.

On June 3, 1982, Palestinian operatives attempted to assassinate Israel's ambassador to the United Kingdom, Shlomo Argov. In response, Israel moved to blockade West Beirut, which was occupied by PLO troops, thus preventing the Palestinians from leaving the city. Shortly thereafter, the United States, Britain, Italy, and France, established a peacekeeping constabulary known as the Multinational Force in Lebanon (MNF)—whose purpose was to assist the Lebanese Army in withdrawing PLO, Syrian, and other foreign combatants from Beirut. As with most peacekeeping forces, the MNF were not allowed to engage in combat, except in self-defense.

The F-14 supported the MNF operations mostly through Combat Air Patrols and reconnaissance missions. Operating primarily from the carriers *Eisenhower* and *Kennedy*, the Tomcats assigned to support the MNF conducted daily Tactical Airborne Reconnaissance Pod System (TARPS) missions. The TARPS system was a 17-foot pod containing multiple, highly-sophisticated cameras carried on the plane's starboard side, between the engine nacelles. The pod had four stations, each with different cameras. Each camera had a different functionality: low-altitude, infrared, varying angles, and panoramic views. It was through these TARPS missions that the Tomcat proved its versatility in a non-combat role. After returning from a reconnaissance mission, the film from the on-board camera was hurriedly delivered to the ship's processing station and printed for review. In fact, the shipboard record for TARPS film processing, from carrier landing to prints ready, was 13 minutes. Afterwards, 3,350 feet of new film would be loaded into the TARPS before the Tomcat was airborne on another reconnaissance mission.

The primary goal of the TARPS missions was to locate artillery batteries and determine target intelligence for offshore naval gunfire. While innocuous by nature, it was during one of these daily missions in December 1983 that two F-14s from the *Kennedy* were engaged by Syrian anti-aircraft guns and ten surface-to-air missiles (SAMs). While the two Tomcats evaded enemy ground fire, the US was none too pleased by the encounter with Syria. Thus, on December 4, 1983, a retaliatory strike force went aloft with twelve

An F-14 from Squadron VF-21 "Free Lancers" takes off from the USS *Constellation* during fleet maneuvers on October 29, 1984. Throughout the decade, the F-14 would prove itself as a viable air asset during the "hot spot" contingency missions in the Caribbean and the Middle East. (US Navy)

An F-14 from Squadron VF-33 "Starfighters," launches from the flight deck of the USS *America* during Exercise *Ocean Safari '85*. (US Navy)

A-7 Corsairs, sixteen A-6 Intruders, one E-2 Hawkeye, two EA-6 Prowlers, and two F-14s. Their mission was to attack an ammunition depot, selected air defense radars, anti-aircraft guns, and surface-to-air missile sites. Although the strike force hit fourteen of its twenty identified targets, one A-6 and one A-7 were lost to enemy fire. The A-6 crew was killed, but the A-7 Corsair pilot safely ejected and was later rescued.

For the F-14, most encounters with the Syrian Air Force ended with no confrontation. Indeed, these Syrian MiGs responded to the F-14s with abortive maneuvers and evasion—seemingly having no desire to tangle with American Tomcats.

Grenada

On October 25, 1983, American forces invaded the 130-square-mile island of Grenada. Off the northern coast of Venezuela in the Caribbean Sea, Grenada had become a hotbed of communist activity. The rise of the so-called New Jewel Movement had precipitated an armed takeover of the island government in 1979. The new Marxist-Leninist regime (under the leadership of Maurice Bishop) suspended the constitution, announced the creation of a new People's Revolutionary Government, and formed a close partnership with Communist Cuba. Within a few years, however, the country's economic hardships led to a coup d'état by Deputy Prime Minister Bernard Coard. In 1983, Coard loyalists forced Bishop under house arrest and executed him shortly thereafter. Grenada then formed a new military government, the Revolutionary Military Council. Unsettled by Coard's behavior, and troubled by the apparent "Soviet-Cuban militarization" of the

Caribbean, the Reagan Administration decided to intervene militarily.

Code-named Operation Urgent Fury, the invasion also sought to prevent a repeat of the Iran hostage crisis. With a pro-Soviet, pro-Cuban, pro-communist coup d'état erupting on a nearby Caribbean island, the threat was such that the US could not ignore. With some 600 American medical students on the island, the number of US civilians in Grenada was higher than it had been in Iran during the Islamic Revolution.

The invasion of Grenada was a fast and furious *tour-de-force*. From the United States, troops from the Army's Rapid Deployment Force (1st and 2d Ranger Battalions and the 82d Airborne Division), Army Delta Force, 22d Marine Amphibious Unit, and Navy SEALS formed the backbone of the ground attack force. From the air, US Navy and Air Force fighter jets provided various levels of support.

The F–14s assigned to Urgent Fury operated from the USS *Independence*, wherein they made extensive use of their TARPS systems and patrolled the island, vigilant for any suspicious aircraft. Using the on-board TARPS, the F–14s provided both pre- and post-invasion support. They flew initial night reconnaissance over the island to photograph enemy targets, which were then delivered to ground commanders prior to the invasion. Following the invasion, F–14s conducted several flyovers to assess the post-strike damage.

Within three days of the invasion, the Cuban-Grenadian resistance had collapsed and the American medical students had been evacuated. Following the US victory, an interim government was put in place pending new elections the following year. In December 1984, the Grenada National Party won the postwar elections, re-establishing Grenada as a parliamentary democracy, which it remains to this day.

A Tomcat from Squadron VF-74 lands aboard the USS *Saratoga* during its deployment to the Mediterranean, September 1985. During this deployment, the Tomcats from VF-74 were called upon to interdict the Egyptian Boeing 737 carrying the perpetrators of the *Achille Lauro* Incident. (US Navy)

Achille Lauro Incident

On October 7, 1985, the Italian cruise ship *Achille Lauro* was sailing from Alexandria to Port Said, Egypt en route to Ashdod, Israel. Unbeknownst to the crew, however, the passenger manifest included four members of the Palestinian Liberation Front (PLF) who were planning to use the *Achille Lauro* as a bargaining chip. Hijacking the ocean liner that afternoon, the four militants took the passengers and crew hostage. Directing the vessel to sail to Tartus, Syria, the PLF terrorists demanded the release of 50 Palestinian prisoners being held in Israel.

By 1985, Palestinian acts of terror were nothing new. Ever since the hostage crisis at the 1972 Olympics in Munich, the West had grown somewhat accustomed to the occasional bouts of Palestinian strife manifesting itself in the form of terrorism.

This time, however, the terror tactics had risen to a new level.

These PLF commandos had not only hijacked a ship full of innocent people, they had also savagely murdered an American citizen, Leon Klinghoffer, a retired businessman who was bound to a wheelchair. Dumping his body overboard, Klinghoffer's corpse later washed ashore on the beaches of Syria. After two days of negotiation, the terrorists agreed to abandon the vessel in exchange for safe passage to Tunisia aboard an Egyptian airliner. Using a chartered Egypt Air Boeing 737, the four PLF members would fly from Cairo to Tunis, where they would presumably be turned over to the Palestine Liberation Organization (PLO), then headed by Yasser Arafat.

Another Tomcat Squadron VF-74 lands on the *Saratoga* during flight operations in the Mediterranean Sea on February 12, 1986. On this same deployment as the *Achille Lauro* Incident, VF-74 would also participate in Operation El Dorado Canyon, the bombing campaign against Muammar al-Gaddafi in Libya. (US Navy)

US Navy aircraft prepare to launch from the USS *America* during Operation El Dorado Canyon on April 15, 1986. In the foreground stands an F-14 from Squadron VF-102 "Diamondbacks." (US Navy)

Outraged by this senseless act of violence—and outraged that the Egyptian government had co-opted to sequester these militants—President Ronald Reagan authorized a plan to intercept the commercial airliner and force its landing onto a nearby NATO enclave.

While the *Achille Lauro* affair unfolded off the coast of Egypt, the carrier USS *Saratoga* was participating in the NATO exercise Display Determination. It was just another naval exercise until the Carrier Task Force commander, Rear Admiral David Jeremiah, received word of the *Achille Lauro's* distress. Subsequently, Commander Robert "Bubba" Brodzky, the commanding officer of Carrier Air Wing 17, developed the plan to intercept the Egyptian airliner using F-14s from Squadrons VF-74 and VF-103. Assisting the Tomcats on this intercept mission would be an E-2 Hawkeye from Squadron VAW-125; two KA-6D aerial refueling tankers from Squadron VA-85; and an EA-6B Prowler from Squadron VAQ-137. An additional E-2 Hawkeye, along with two additional electronic warfare planes—one EA-3B and an EC-135—would accompany the task force for its interception of the Egypt Air flight.

On the night of October 10, 1985, the first cluster of aircraft catapulted from the flight deck aboard the *Saratoga*. The F-14s were airborne just as the Egyptian airliner left the tarmac at Cairo International Airport. Although the F-14s would be the "muscle" for this nighttime intercept, the accompanying aircraft would be the Tomcats' "eyes and ears." The EA-6B, for example, would jam all transmissions from the Egyptian 737 if it tried

On April 17, 1986, two days after Operation El Dorado Canyon, it was back to "business as usual" on the flight decks on the USS *America*. Here, an F-14 from Squadron VF-33 (left), and a KA-6D Intruder from Squadron VA-34 (right) prepare to launch for their normal "day-cyclic" flight operations off the coast of Libya. (US Navy)

to communicate with other stations. The E-2 Hawkeyes, meanwhile, would guide the F-14s onto the 737 while scanning the surrounding area for any unwelcomed aircraft. The EC-135, a US Air Force asset with onboard Arab interpreters, would monitor and translate any radio traffic made to or from the Egyptian Air flight. All told, the task force's mission was clear: intercept the 737 before it landed in Tunis.

Lumbering into the night, the American planes approached their target while flying "lights out"—meaning that the F-14s had turned off their running lights so as not to alert the Egyptian air crew of their presence. Thus, to positively identify the Egyptian 737, the Tomcat pilots had to use handheld flashlights to shine upon the airliner's tail number. This required the Tomcat pilots to fly within a mere *fifteen feet* of the 737's fuselage to gain positive identification.

To this day, the names of the F-14 pilots remain classified due to security reasons. However, the anonymous pilot of the F-14 *Slugger 205*, approached the Egyptian airliner from the rear and, using his flashlight technique, positively identified it as the 737 carrying the Palestinian fugitives.

Moments later, the E-2C scrambled five additional Tomcats (though some sources indicate it was only three) to assist with the intercept. As the other Tomcats joined the "lights out" formation, the E-2C made its first appeal to the Egyptian 737 on a VHF frequency. The E-2C identified itself as a US Navy aircraft and ordered the 737 crew to divert themselves to NATO Base Sigonella in Sicily. All the while, the Egyptian crew remained unaware that a flight of fully-armed F-14s lingered just a few meters behind their aircraft.

Under obvious duress from the on-board Palestinians, the Egyptian air crew refused the order. Having no luck in coaxing the 737's compliance, the E-2 then directed all seven F-14s to move onto either side of the airliner.

On the command, "Lights on, NOW!," the seven Tomcats ignited their running lights.

The sudden appearance of seven simultaneous F-14s sent the Egyptian airmen into a panic. Indeed, the F-14 pilots recalled seeing the Egyptian aircrew and the Palestinian passengers running helter-skelter along the inside of the fuselage, peering through the airliner's windows with looks of terror and frustration. Once again, the Hawkeye instructed the Boeing 737 to proceed to Sigonella.

This time, the Egyptian airmen complied.

Once the 737 touched down at Sigonella, the Tomcats closed off the surrounding airspace for all incoming aircraft. The Egyptian airliner was then quickly surrounded by Italian military police. Although the US attempted to have the hijackers extradited to stand trial in America, the four militants remained in Italian custody. At their Italian trial, three of the four PLA militants received prison sentences ranging from 15–30 years.

Although many decried the Italian ruling as soft-handed justice, the *Achille Lauro* Incident showcased how well the US could employ air power as a tool for antiterrorism. The F-14's role in the operation stood as a testament to its versatility and resilience as a contingency air asset.

Further Action in the Gulf of Sidra

After the Gulf of Sidra Incident in 1981, the US kept a close eye on Libya. Despite losing a pair of Sukhoi Su-22s in a humiliating dogfight, Muammar al-Gaddafi showed no signs of curtailing his rhetoric. From his support of terrorist groups, to his attempts at nuclear

Towards the end of its deployment in the Mediterranean, a Tomcat from VF-74 prepares for another Combat Air Patrol in the summer of 1986. (US Navy)

An F-14 Tomcat from Squadron VF-154 "Black Knights" is readied for launch on Catapult 3 aboard the USS *Constellation* in the Indian Ocean on July 1, 1987. (US Navy)

power, and his insistence on the nautical "Line of Death," Gaddafi was becoming a threat that the US could no longer ignore.

Tensions escalated further on the morning of March 23, 1986 when two F-14s from Squadron VF-102 "Diamondbacks" (flying from the USS *America*) crossed the imaginary "Line of Death" and were engaged by two Libyan surface-to-air missiles. The missiles, fired from the air defense station near Surt, missed the Tomcats and fell harmlessly into the Mediterranean. Undeterred, the Libyans fired two more missiles, but they were quickly jammed by a nearby EA-6B Prowler.

Shortly before 10:00 AM, two Libyan MiG-23s took off from Benina Air Base with orders to shoot down any US fighters in the area. As the MiGs took off, however, an E-2 Hawkeye detected them on radar and alerted Squadron VF-33 "Starfighters" to intercept. Fortunately, VF-33 already had two Tomcats in the air—and the F-14s happily answered the call. Meeting the MiG-23s at an altitude of 20,000 feet, the Tomcats vectored to avoid the aggressive head-on maneuvers of the incoming bandits. As the MiGs' hostile intent was clear, the Battle Group Commander radioed the Tomcats: "Warning Yellow; Weapons Hold," meaning that the F-14s could fire if necessary.

As the Tomcats gave chase, they descended to 5,000 feet, where they would have a distinct advantage over the MiG-23s. Indeed, the MiG-23 was ill-equipped to engage in low-level dogfights. Both Tomcats sallied into the six o' clock position behind their respective MiGs—each getting a missile lock with their AIM-9 Sidewinders. However, before either pilot could depress the trigger, the MiGs broke off and began flying towards the Libyan coast. Thinking that the engagement was over, both Tomcats prepared to finish the remainder of their air patrol until one of the MiGs reversed course. The F-14 flight leader again acquired missile lock on the offending MiG and requested permission to fire. But just then, the prodding MiG-23 turned away and began flying south. Although no shots had been fired during this aerial skirmish, it nevertheless underscored the lingering tensions between Libya and the US.

Aside from his unabashed support of terrorism, Gaddafi himself had orchestrated a number of terror plots. One such occurrence was the bombing of a West Berlin nightclub by Libyan agents on April 5, 1986. Three people were killed, including a US serviceman; 299 were injured—63 of whom were American.

Almost simultaneously, the Reagan Administration began researching potential targets for a strike on Libya. The goal was to decimate Gaddafi's terrorist infrastructure, disrupt his internal operations, and deplete his military resources. Of the possible 152 targets, five were ultimately selected:

1. Murat Sidi Bilal, in Tripoli - a training camp and school for naval commandos and terrorist frogmen.

2. Tripoli International Airport - the base for nine Ilyushin Il-76 transports that had supported terrorist activity.

3. Jamhuriya Guard Barracks, in Benghazi - a terrorist command center.

4. The Bab al-Aziziya complex, in Tripoli - Gaddafi's compound, headquarters and main residence.

5. Benina Air Force Base, outside Benghazi - Maintenance and storage facilities for MiG-23s flown by Syria, PLO, and North Korea.

In all, President Reagan saw the West Berlin nightclub as a direct attack on the United States. "Self-defense is not only our right," he said, "it is our duty." Invoking international law, Reagan said: "It is the purpose behind the mission...a mission fully consistent with Article 51 of the UN Charter." Reagan wanted to hit Gaddafi where it would hurt the most. And although Reagan didn't intend for this operation to be a direct assassination attempt, he nevertheless knew it would leave a devastating impact.

To affect the element of surprise, minimize civilian casualties, and attack the Libyan defenses at their lowest ebb, the US decided to launch Operation El Dorado Canyon at night. Thus, in the pre-dawn hours of April 14, 1986, the first American sorties launched from the flight decks of the USS *America* and USS *Coral Sea*. The F-14s from Squadrons VF-33 and VF-102 flew into battle alongside A-6 Intruders and Air Force F-111 Aardvarks, followed closely by KC-10A and KC-135 aerial refuelers.

The F-111Es vectored to engage the Tripoli targets, while the A-6Es attacked Benghazi. The Tomcats' mission was to escort the F-111Es to Tripoli and dissuade any defending aircraft. In a strange turn of events, however, the Tomcats' first encounter of the day involved not Libyans, but Italians. Indeed, the Italian Air Force had detected the incoming armada of F-111s and scrambled a flight of F-104 Starfighters to investigate. Upon approaching the large group of American aircraft, Italian pilot Major Giorgia

A VF-33 Tomcat launches from the deck of the USS *Theodore Roosevelt* in the Atlantic Ocean on September 30, 1987. (US Navy)

Riolo explains, "We saw them for the first time from a range of about 20 miles. There was a long trail of navigation lights—which turned out to be several KC-135s. Before long, we found ourselves underway in the middle of a huge airborne armada, with unknown aircraft all around us. I informed our GCI [Ground Control Interception radar station] and decided to leave the area. The few other Starfighters scrambled with similar orders to inspect were aggressively approached by F-14s of the US Navy that asked them to move away-immediately."

After this encounter, and despite being a US ally, the Italian government alerted Libya of the incoming attack. Whatever their motives may have been, the Italians succeeded in alerting Gaddafi at his Bab al-Aziziya residence only minutes before the F-111s arrived.

The Libyan leader barely escaped with his family.

However, even if Gaddafi had remained at his compound, it's unlikely that the F-111 strike would have killed him. In fact, of the dozen or so bombs released over Gaddafi's residence, none scored a direct hit. Instead, they landed between a ceremonial tent and an administration building. The bombs collapsed a few walls, caved in roofs, and shattered several windows, but otherwise left the compound unscathed.

In Benghazi, the A-6Es had a similar arrival. Flying under radio silence, the A-6 pilots caught Libyan forces at Benghazi completely by surprise. According to one US serviceman: "With the lights on you could see the targets just where they were supposed to be." It was later discovered that the Libyan radars did, in fact, detect the incoming American planes. However, the radar technicians were so poorly trained that they did not recognize the incoming flights as a threat. Moreover, communication between the early-warning radar stations and the air defense sites was lacking. With little to no deterrence, the A-6E Intruders vectored into Benghazi, dropping at least sixty CBU-59

Aircraft handlers aboard the USS *Carl Vinson* brush snow and ice off the wings of three F-14s belonging to Squadron VF-111 "Sundowners" during operations in the Western Pacific, January 1987. (US Navy)

cluster bombs along Benina Air Base—destroying the runway, several MiG-23s, two Mi-8 helicopters, an Aeritalia G.222 transport, a Boeing 727, and an SF.260 trainer. The sortie against Jamhuriya Barracks produced similar results, destroying nearby warehouses with MiG-23 parts.

After the success of the aerial bombardment, the US squadrons returned to the safety of international airspace. The F-14s from the USS *America* remained in the sky conducting combat air patrols. Their job was to monitor the coastal airspace and prevent any Libyan interceptors from attacking the returning American aircraft. According to RIO Lieutenant Dave Parsons, "The F-14s had a grandstand view of all the fireworks and was hoping some Libyan interceptor would approach. But nothing happened so they deloused everybody coming out and stayed south until all packages were recovered."

The Tanker War

As the Iran-Iraq War raged into its final years, Saddam Hussein grew increasingly frustrated by his inability to conquer the Iranians. Having made little progress on the ground, or in the air, Saddam shifted his focus into the waters of the Persian Gulf. If he could not conquer Iran by air or land, he would disrupt their shipping operations on the near seas; indeed, he would begin targeting their shipping lines and oil tankers. Thus began the so-called "Tanker War."

Saddam's intent was to provoke Iran into closing the Strait of Hormuz, a critical trade passage that handled twenty percent of the world's petroleum shipping. By forcing the Strait closed, a retaliatory response from the West would certainly help the Iraqi war effort.

In a recurring episode throughout the latter decades of the Cold War, this F-14 Tomcat intercepts a Tupelov Tu-95 "Bear" of the Soviet Navy. October 1985. During these high-seas intercepts, the Tu-95 was the most frequent visitor. (US Navy)

Iran, however, didn't take the bait.

Leaving the Strait of Hormuz open, Iran stated it would attack all ships found in the northern zone of the Persian Gulf. As the attacks increased, Iran and Iraq used their air forces to sweep the seas for any oil tankers. During these back-and-forth engagements, the Iraqi Air Force struck Khark Island, Iran's main oil export facility. The Tanker War officially started in 1984, with the Iraqi Air Force and the IRIAF attacking any oil vessel they found in the Gulf—including ships from Kuwait and Saudi Arabia. Due to the unbiased nature of these attacks, the Kuwaiti government solicited US naval protection for their oil tankers. The US, while already supporting Iraq in its war against the Ayatollah Khomeini, worried about the impact that this Iran-Iraq conflict might have on oil exports. Therefore, to ease the situation, the United States moved forward with Operation Earnest Will, a naval escort mission to protect Kuwaiti tankers passing through the Persian Gulf. As part of the operation, Kuwaiti vessels had to register and fly the American flag, due to the legal requirements for a civilian freighter to receive naval protection.

Operation Earnest Will began on July 23, 1987—sadly with lackluster results. The United States protection of Kuwaiti tankers involved Navy warships including aircraft carriers, frigates, cruisers, and destroyers. As part of their mission, the carriers provided aerial cover via their squadrons of A-6 Intruders, F/A-18 Hornets, EA-6B Prowlers, and

F–14 Tomcats. Their first mission—protecting the SS *Bridgton* supertanker—demonstrated that the naval task force was missing one critical asset: a minesweeper. Midway through the journey, the *Bridgeton* struck an underwater mine, causing significant damage to the tanker. Although there were no casualties, and the ship was able to continue its journey, it nevertheless highlighted the perils of the escort mission.

While Iranian F–14s blasted away at Iraqi targets elsewhere in the Persian Gulf, American Tomcats supported the escort mission by patrolling the nearby airspace for their Iranian counterparts, or any other approaching threat. The biggest incident for American F–14s occurred on August 8, 1987, while flying a Combat Air Patrol from the USS *Constellation*. Two F–14s from Squadron VF-21 spotted two Iranian F-4s approaching an American P-3C Orion running reconnaissance. As the Iranian F-4s moved within range, the two Tomcats fired their AIM-7 Sparrow missiles. As the missiles approached their intended targets, however, the Tomcats vectored away and did not confirm if the Sparrows had hit the Iranian bandits. As it turned out, one missile had malfunctioned and plummeted into the sea, while the other was evaded. Months later, on April 18, 1988, Iranian F-4s tried to intercept an E-2 Hawkeye flying from the USS *Enterprise*. Luckily for the E-2, the would-be bandits were warned off by a pair of Tomcats from Squadron VF-213.

Beyond these engagements, the rest of the Tanker War was relatively uneventful for the F–14s—providing aerial cover, roving patrol, and escort services to allied vessels in the Persian Gulf.

An F-14 from Squadron VF-1 "Wolfpack" escorting two Soviet Tupolev Tu-16 "Badgers" away from the carrier USS *Kitty Hawk's* operational area. Most of these intercepts, and subsequent escorts, ended without confrontation. In fact, many pilots recalled these intercepts as humorous encounters. On one occasion, an American pilot recalled a Soviet air crewman waving a "peep show" magazine at him. (US Navy)

Not all intercepts on the high seas involved potential enemies. Occasionally, the air forces of allied nations would vector too close to the US carrier group, necessitating an escort. Such was the case here, in November 1981, when this F-14 Tomcat from Squadron VF-213 intercepted an Il-38 from the Indian Navy. (US Navy)

Close Encounters in the Pacific

Throughout the 1980s, US carrier forces frequently encountered Soviet aircraft on the high seas or near the territorial waters of the American coastline. The most common perpetrator was the Tupelov Tu-95 "Bear" flying reconnaissance. While many of these encounters occurred on the high seas, it was seldom that they occurred in potentially hostile waters. Yet such was the case on August 14, 1987, when F-14s from a carrier battle group encountered Soviet MiGs off the coast of Vietnam.

Aboard the USS *Ranger*, sailors and flight crews prepared to rendezvous with the USS *Constellation* and the USS *New Jersey* for what would be a large-scale naval exercise in the Pacific. En route to this large rendezvous, however, the *Ranger's* air squadron, VF-2 "Bounty Hunters," intercepted a large number of Soviet MiG-23s flying from Cam Rahn Air Base, Vietnam. Cam Rahn had previously been an American air station during the Vietnam War. After the fall of Saigon, the Communist regime leased the facility to the Soviet Navy and Soviet Air Force until 1989.

On this hot summer day in 1987, Lieutenant Jon "Hooter" Schreiber was a ten-year naval aviator then-assigned to Squadron VF-2. To this point, Schreiber, like many of his comrades, had intercepted several Soviet-made reconnaissance aircraft—including the Tu-95 and Il-38. While flying CAP around the carrier group's maneuver space, these close encounters usually followed a predictable pattern. "In many cases," Schreiber said, "the bogie turned away before getting to the battle group. Indeed, I only saw one 'Bear'

In this photograph, another F-14 from Squadron VF-213 intercepts an Iranian Lockheed P-3F Orion over the Indian Ocean. Although the US and Iran were no longer allies, the IRIAF retained much of the American aircraft they had purchased during the reign of the Shah. (US Navy)

[Tu-95] fly by the ship in the three cruises that I made." On another occasion, Schreiber escorted an Indian Navy Il-38 patrol aircraft away from the carrier group. The Soviet-made Il-38 was the Warsaw Pact's equivalent to the P-3 Orion. Of course, the Indian Navy had no hostile intent, but the presence of an Il-38 underscored the depth of the Soviet arms trade. "During my time flying the F-14," he continued, "I escorted an An-12 'Cub' transport, but it did not fly by the ship. Neither the Il-38 nor the An-12 were considered terribly threatening. I was once vectored on to a couple of Tu-16 'Badgers,' but the weather was so bad we never saw them."

Thus, on the morning of August 14, Schreiber hadn't expected to see anything beyond the typical Soviet reconnaissance fare. That day, Schreiber was piloting the F-14 call-signed *Bullet 200* with Commander Jim "Thumb Dog" Dodge as his RIO. Coincidentally, Dodge was also the Squadron Commander. "We started our Tomcat, went through our checks and were airborne in less than 5 minutes," Schreiber recalled. "We were told that there was a MiG-23 'Flogger'…headed towards the ship. I was excited to be actually launching on a threat." Indeed, Schreiber and Dodge welcomed this unexpected change to the monotony of their aerial interceptions. Not many pilots had seen a MiG-23 up close, much less a MiG-23 piloted by a Soviet aviator. "Since we were operating under peacetime ROE [Rules of Engagement], our only mission was to keep the bogey from flying near the ship unescorted. We would not shoot it down if it decided to fly over the ship, unless it did something very provocative." Essentially, the Rules of Engagement said not to fire unless fired upon.

When *Bullet 200* launched from the flight deck, the plane was about 100 miles due east of Cam Ranh. Shortly after take-off, Dodge picked up the radar signature of a bogey (presumably the MiG) at a distance of 20 miles. At their current airspeed, *Bullet 200* would intercept the bogey in about one minute. As Schreiber maneuvered his F–14 to intercept, he took pause to admire the surroundings. Despite the tropical weather, the sky was overcast, and he remarked that the ocean looked more gray than blue. "To the west," he recalled, "I could make out the verdant mountains of Vietnam breaking the monotony of gray sea and gray sky. The overcast was actually a nice environmental element that would take sun glare and sea glint out of the engagement calculus."

At an altitude of 5,000 feet, *Bullet 200* passed the MiG-23 head-on, going in the opposite direction. Seemingly startled by the appearance of an American F-14, the MiG pilot broke right, vectoring upward. Schreiber continued left and pulled up, hoping to get an altitude advantage and descend behind the MiG. "After about 180 degrees of turn, I passed about 1,000 feet above the bogie, a little aft of his wing line. This was going well. The 'Flogger' reversed again and I continued to roll through about three-quarters of an aileron roll and pulled back into him now in a right-hand turn." After a few more turns, Schreiber recalled that "the bogey just kind of stopped playing," and levelled his plane on a flight path back to the mainland.

A Soviet MiG-23 "Flogger" flying from the Soviet air base in Cam Rahn Bay, Vietnam. This is a MiG similar to the one that intercepted Lieutenant Jon "Hooter" Schreiber off the coast of Vietnam on August 14, 1987. While most intercepts featured the Tupelov-series aircraft, and its associated contemporaries, it was rare that an American pilot encountered a MiG-23 piloted by a Soviet aviator. (US Department of Defense)

Not all intercepts involved aircraft. Some pilots encounter Soviet Navy ships, such as this *Balzam*-class surveillance vessel, found off the coast of Virginia in September 1985. As seen from the photograph, this F-14 Tomcat from Squadron VF-102 runs interference to ensure that the Soviet vessel does not violate America's territorial waters. (US Navy)

But *Bullet 200* wasn't done yet.

Now that they had seen a Soviet MiG up close, Schreiber and Dodge wanted a photo opportunity. "The Skipper and I rolled out and tried to join up as the 'Flogger' appeared to be heading back to base. We made sure that we were not going to violate the 12-mile airspace limit surrounding the coast of Vietnam and cause some sort of political incident. We double-checked our position with the E-2C Hawkeye and the ship, both of which were keeping us aware of our geographic location and other potential threats in the area." For example, another F-14 from their squadron was escorting a different MiG-23 several miles north of Schreiber and Dodge's location.

As *Bullet 200* got closer to the fleeting MiG, Schreiber and Dodge readied their camera for a close-up. Typically, these photo sessions were light-hearted moments, and both sides regularly participated. Today, however, this MiG-23 pilot was in no mood for the customary photo antics. "He began modulating his thrust from [afterburner] to idle, deploying and retracting his speed brakes and flapping his wing spoilers and elevons up and down like he was sending us semaphore [naval flag] signals."

Essentially, the MiG pilot was telling Schreiber to back off.

Not wanting to push the situation, or wander into Vietnamese airspace, *Bullet 200* broke off its pursuit and headed back towards the flight deck. Moments later, however, the E-2C radioed that the same MiG was now returning in the direction of the ship. Vectoring to re-engage the MiG, Schreiber and the Soviet pilot re-played the same choreography they had done .minutes earlier—a head-on pass, followed by a short pursuit to the edge of Vietnam's airspace. After the MiG-23 descended into its home airspace, *Bullet 200* once again broke off the chase and vectored back towards the *Ranger*. However, for a third time, the MiG-23 reversed itself and began barreling back towards the carrier group. Growing tired of this cat-and-mouse game, Schreiber and Dodge aggressively descended upon the MiG, this time getting close enough to see the Soviet pilot's face. Schreiber's most poignant recollection from this third encounter was seeing the Russian pilot's exotic moustache. Perhaps shaken by the F-14's proximity to his own cockpit, the MiG-23 pilot quickly yielded the airspace to *Bullet 200* and returned to Cam Rahn.

Another close encounter between American F-14s and Soviet MiG-23s occurred a few months later on February 8, 1988. Aboard the USS *Enterprise*, Carrier Air Wing 11 was embarked on another cruise, navigating through the South China Sea with Squadrons VF-114 "Aardvarks" and VF-213 "Blacklions." Per usual, VF-114 and VF-213 had planned to send up their normal variety of Combat Air Patrols. On that morning of February 8, *Lion 200* from VF-213, piloted by Lieutenant Darhl "Snail" Ehrgott and his RIO Lieutenant Dave "Swobes" Swoboda, sat on the catapult ready for take-off.

Suddenly, an E-2C Hawkeye from Squadron VAW-117 "Wallbangers" notified the *Enterprise* of an inbound bogey closing in from a distance of 115 miles. Responding to the call, Ehrgott and Swoboda launched from the flight deck, ready to meet the lurking bandit on the horizon. Upon gaining visual, Erghott quickly determined that the offending aircraft was a MiG-23. Climbing to meet the Flogger, *Lion 200* hastily intercepted the prowling MiG-23. Watching the MiG's poor handling and erratic maneuvers, however, Ehrgott quickly deduced that the Soviet pilot was a rookie. Indeed, this MiG pilot made several maneuvering mistakes typical of unseasoned pilots fresh from flight school. At one point during the chase, the Soviet flyer dove into the clouds, trying to shake the pursuing Tomcat. Biding their time, Ehrgott and Swoboda waited for the MiG to exit the clouds and immediately resumed the chase. After six more attempts to evade his American pursuers, the MiG-23 began to run out of fuel. It dove into the clouds one final time, before flying back to Cam Ranh Bay. After *Lion 200* refueled from an aerial tanker, Ehrgott and Swoboda were vectored onto another MiG-23 that had been detected in the area. Intercepting the second MiG-23, Ehrgott maneuvered *Lion 200* within twenty-five feet below the MiG's fuselage and took pictures of its missile package before returning to the *Enterprise*.

Gulf of Sidra Incident, 1989

Eight years after the first Gulf of Sidra Incident in 1981, American Tomcats met the Libyan Air Force in a contest of fire once again. This time, the aggressors were a pair of Libyan MiG-23s. Following the first engagement near Gaddafi's "Line of Death," US-Libyan relations had gone from bad to worse. Despite his humiliating defeat during Operation *El Dorado Canyon*, Colonel Gaddafi had doubled down on his efforts to expand Libya's military and build his chemical arsenal. His aggressive expansion into the realm of chemical weapons precipitated the second Gulf of Sidra Incident in January 1989.

In the fall of 1988, the Gaddafi regime began construction of a chemical plant near Rabta, Libya. Western analysts believed that the chemical plant was being fitted for mustard gas production. Libya, however, denied this claim—stating that the facility was simply a pharmaceutical plant. Already suspicious of the Gaddafi regime and its reckless behavior, President Ronald Reagan publicly warned the international community about

Embarked upon the USS *John F. Kennedy,* this Tomcat from Squadron VF-14 prepares to launch from the carrier deck on its deployment to the Mediterranean, January 1989. As part of Carrier Air Wing 3, Squadrons VF-14 and VF-32 patrolled various parts of the Mediterranean Sea—including the Gulf of Sidra, where Libyan leader Muammar al-Gaddafi held fast to his foolhardy "Line of Death." (US Navy)

Gypsy 207 (foreground), one of two American F-14s that engaged Libyan MiG-23s on January 4, 1989, in what became the Second Gulf of Sidra Incident. (US Navy)

Libya's intentions. In fact, during a press conference in December 1988, President Reagan declared that he wouldn't hesitate to destroy the chemical plant if necessary.

Coincidentally, on January 1, 1989, the USS *John F Kennedy* departed from Cannes, France, sailing towards Haifa, Israel on a course 120 miles north of Libya. This short cruise into the Mediterranean would include the normal variety of carrier-based air patrols—involving both E-2 Hawkeyes and F-14 Tomcats. Officially, these exercises were deemed "non-provocative" and "day-cyclic" operations; but the presence of the US naval carriers had put Gaddafi on edge. According to Les Aspin, Chairman of the House Armed Services Committee, the memories of *El Dorado Canyon* and President Reagan's recent remarks had prompted Gaddafi to begin fortifying Libya's coastal and air defenses—later noting that "Gaddafi has been notoriously paranoid in recent days about some kind of American attack, and the Libyan military has been more active than usual."

On the morning of January 4, 1989, Squadron VF-32 "Fighting Swordsmen" readied two Tomcats on the flight deck of the *Kennedy*. The lead Tomcat, *Gypsy 207*, was piloted by Commander Joseph B. Connelly, the commanding officer of VF-32; his Radar Intercept Officer (RIO) was Commander Leo Enwright. The second Tomcat, *Gypsy 202*, was piloted by Lieutenant Herman Cook, with Lieutenant Commander Steven Collins as his RIO. Simultaneously, Squadron VF-14 "Tophatters" sent two additional F-14s to occupy another sector of the same patrol area.

The Carrier Air Wing had expected this mission to be nothing more than a routine air patrol. However, given their proximity to the Libyan coast, American flight commanders had cause for concern. Before takeoff, the crews of *Gypsy 207* and *Gypsy 202* had been instructed to take warning of any Libyan aircraft. Although the Libyans had not engaged US forces since 1986, tensions remained high and the recent rhetoric regarding the Rabta chemical plant had put Gaddafi on high alert. Consequently, the Libyan Air Force had moved more of its MiG squadrons to the airbases at Al Bumbah and Gamel Abdel Nassar, both of which had easy access to the Gulf of Sidra.

To this point, it had been a long-standing policy for the US Navy to send only its most-experienced aircrews on patrols near Libyan waters. For this particular cruise, however, the carrier group commander recommended the air squadrons send at least one "nugget" (i.e. novice) aircrew towards the Libyan frontier so they could gain experience flying in that region. Thus, of the two Tomcats in each section, one plane would have a "nugget" pilot with an experienced RIO, while the other plane would have an experienced pilot with a "nugget" RIO.

Beyond their advisory of a potential encounter with Libyan aircraft, Connelly and Cook also received the latest revision to the Rules of Engagement (ROE). In years past, ROEs typically stated "Do not fire unless fired upon." However, new advancements in aviation technology had rendered these rules obsolete. Indeed, these newer technologies now permitted an enemy to attack from a greater distance, in any direction, and often without warning. According to J. Daniel Howard, the US Department of Defense spokesman at the time, "The rules have been gradually amended to give the guy in the cockpit more flexibility to defend himself when he thinks there is hostile intent. You can no longer afford to wait to be fired on."

With this in mind, *Gypsy 207* and *Gypsy 202* took off from the flight deck at 11:30 that morning, armed with four AIM-7 Sparrows and two AIM-9 Sidewinders. The two Tomcats from Squadron VF-32 then vectored to the eastern sector of their assigned Combat Air Patrol. Meanwhile, their counterparts in Squadron VF-14 occupied the

Practicing a missile shot over the Mediterranean, this F-14 Tomcat from VF-32 hones its skills for aerial combat. Although the Carrier Air Wing had not anticipated any hostilities in the Gulf of Sidra, tensions between the US and Libya remained high, and the F-14s were advised to be on alert. (US Navy)

western sector. Shortly after takeoff, Commander Enwright's on-board radar began to malfunction. No surprises there; the F-14's radar was a temperamental machine, and the RIO often had to reboot it during flight. Such was the case when Enwright turned off his radar, re-starting it just in time to receive a critical call from a nearby surveillance plane.

At 11:55 AM, an E-2 Hawkeye from Squadron VAW-126 "Seahawks" radioed *Gypsy 207*, informing Connelly that two MiG-23 "Floggers" had taken off from the Al Bumbah Air Base, near Tobruk. Based on their projected flight patterns, the Hawkeye determined that these MiGs were headed towards the eastern sector of the American air patrol. When Commander Connelly received the call, he and Lieutenant Cook were nearly 80 miles from the Libyan coast. As the two F-14s vectored to intercept, they detected the incoming bogeys on their own radar at seventy-two nautical miles. "Contacts appear to be heading 315 now," radioed Enwright, "speed 430, angels approximately 8,000"— indicating that the incoming bogeys were at an altitude of 8,000 feet.

"Roger, ace," replied the E-2, "take it north."

Normally, Libyan MiGs would depart the scene once they realized they were showing up on an F-14's radar. Today, however, the Libyan bandits decided to stay the course and continued their flight pattern towards *Gypsy 207* and *202*.

"We have to make a quick loop here," said Connelly into the radio.

The F-14s then turned left to conduct a standard intercept. In response, the MiG-23s turned back into the Tomcats, aligning themselves for a head-on approach. Detecting the bogeys' new course, Enwright announced:

"Okay, bogeys appear to be coming, jinking to the right now, heading north."

Around this time, Connelly and Cook began descending from 20,000 to 3,000 feet, to fly lower than the MiGs.

All things considered, Connelly and Cook had little to fear from the incoming MiGs. They knew that the MiG-23s were agile and fast, but these MiGs were likewise small and had a weak radar system, giving their pilots considerable difficulty "detecting and redirecting long-range missiles to low-flying targets."

With these facts in mind, *Gypsy 207* and *Gypsy 202* descended to a lower altitude as a means to reduce the already-limited effectiveness of the MiGs' radar. Moreover, Connelly and Cook wanted to mitigate the effectiveness of the AA-7 Apex missiles that the Libyan MiGs were likely carrying. The AA-7 could be fired from more than ten miles away, and it was one of the most feared air-to-air missiles of its day. The lower altitude would disrupt the MiGs' ability to detect the Tomcats because the ocean clutter would skew the radars' readings.

As the Tomcats descended, Connelly and Cook made another left turn, attempting to evade the Libyan MiGs. However, the prowling MiGs turned as well, maintaining their heading towards *Gypsy 207* and *Gypsy 202*. This time, the MiG-23s increased their speed to 500 knots. Somewhat surprised that these MiGs were *still* pursuing them, Enwright radioed:

"Bogeys have jinked back into us now. Let's go starboard, 30 degrees to the other side."

Upon hearing this transmission, the Battle Group Commander aboard the *Kennedy* replied with "Warning Yellow; Weapons Hold"—authorizing both F-14s to fire on the MiGs if either pilot suspected hostile intent.

Tomcats from Squadron VF-32 prepare to take off from the USS *John F. Kennedy*. Throughout the 1980s, VF-32 saw several deployments aboard the *Kennedy*. (US Navy)

Still, Connelly and Cook wanted to avoid the confrontation if possible—for once a missile was fired, it could never be taken back. Nevertheless, five times *Gypsy 207* and *202* tried to avoid the incoming MiGs, and five times the Libyan bandits vectored to intercept them.

By the fifth time, however, Connelly and Cook had had enough.

"Okay, bogeys have jinked back at me again for the fifth time! They're on my nose now, inside of 20 miles," Connelly bellowed. By now, there could be little doubt that these MiGs were spoiling for a fight. As it turned out, the Floggers were being directed towards the Tomcats' location by a ground radar station at Al Bumbah. Commander Enwright, meanwhile, prepared *Gypsy 207's* missiles for action.

"Master arm on! Master arm on!" he said, arming the on-board Sparrows and Sidewinders.

"Okay, good light, good light," replied Connelly, indicating all systems functional.

By now, the Libyan MiGs were only twelve nautical miles from *Gypsy 207* and *202*. Having acknowledged the Battle Group Commander's earlier authorization for "Weapons Hold," Enwright decided to engage the incoming MiGs. From his RIO position, Enwright fired the first missile of the engagement—sending off an AIM-7 Sparrow.

"Fox One! Fox One!" Enwright shouted, announcing the Sparrow's deployment

"Oh, Jesus!" Connelly cried, as he hadn't expected Enwright to fire.

As the AIM-7 hurtled towards the incoming MiGs, both F-14s executed a defensive split. The first missile failed to track its target, but Connelly maneuvered *Gypsy 207* for another shot. Seemingly unphased by the first Sparrow missile, however, both MiGs continued flying directly towards the F-14s at a speed of 550 knots.

"Breaking Right," Cook announced.

A Soviet MiG-23 "Flogger." Libyan variants of the MiG-23 engaged Tomcats *Gypsy 202* and *Gypsy 207* in the Gulf of Sidra on January 4, 1989. (US Navy)

"Roger that," Connelly replied, "He's back on my nose again," referring to the position of the enemy MiG. "Fox One, again!" said Connelly, firing another missile. But just as the first missile had done, this second missile from *Gypsy 207* missed its target.

Observing the Tomcats' split, both MiGs turned their attention onto *Gypsy 202*, but Cook and his RIO Collins were ready. From his RIO seat, and at a distance of five miles, Collins fired an AIM-7 missile, striking one of the MiGs directly in its right intake duct.

"Good hit, good hit on one!" yelled Cook as he banked the plane hard right.

Meanwhile, Connelly leveled *Gypsy 207* into position behind the remaining MiG as his RIO was shouting, "Select Fox 2 [Sidewinder], Shoot 'em, Fox 2, Fox 2, shoot Fox 2!"

Connelly, however, couldn't get a lock on.

"Shoot him!" cried Enwright.

"I don't got tone," said Connelly.

"Damn, shoot him! Fox 2!"

"I can't, I don't have a f*cking tone!" Connelly bellowed.

Switching back to the Sparrow, Connelly then tried to get tone with the AIM-7, but still to no avail. By now, *Gypsy 207* was closing in fast on the Libyan MiG. Indeed, within a few more seconds, Connelly would be too close for missiles and would have to switch to guns.

Connelly, however, decided to give the AIM-9 one last try.

The volume of the Sidewinder tone nearly drowned out every other sound in the cockpit.

"Tone's up!"

"Fox 2!"

Connelly depressed the trigger and felt the plane rattle as the Sidewinder deployed from its left-wing station. At first, it appeared as though this missile, too, would miss its target. However, Connelly's disappointment quickly turned to relief as he saw the missile arc towards the descending MiG-23. Moments later, the Sidewinder struck the elusive Flogger squarely in its fuselage, just behind the cockpit. As the missile made impact, the Libyan pilot flung open his canopy and ejected from the now-hurtling aircraft.

Less than seven minutes had elapsed from the time Cook and Connelly received the MiG alert. Now, *Gypsy 207* and *202* were reporting both MiGs destroyed, with "two chutes coming down," noting that both enemy pilots had ejected from the crashing Floggers.

Rolling out of their descent at about 700 feet above the sea, Cook and Connelly thrust their engines to 650 knots as they bounded back to the *Kennedy*. Like their comrades eight years earlier, the crews of *Gypsy 207* and *Gypsy 202* were greeted on the flight deck by a thunderous chorus of applause, handshakes, and high fives. As Cook, Connelly, Enwright, and Collins doffed their flight gear in their Squadron Ready Room, they noticed that someone had written on the squadron blackboard, "NAVY FOUR; LIBYA ZERO"—celebrating today's kills and commemorating the pair of Su-22s killed by Muczynski and Kleeman eight years earlier.

Although it was another victory for the US Navy, the political aftermath of this second Gulf of Sidra Incident was more complicated than the first. As President-elect George HW Bush prepared to take the reins in Washington, this latest air battle with Libya

The fuselage of *Gypsy 202*, bearing the silhouette of a generic enemy MiG, denoting that the F-14 pilot had downed an enemy plane in combat. (US Navy)

sparked a debate that lasted well into the 1990s. The true intentions of the Libyan MiGs were never revealed, but Gaddafi claimed that they were only running reconnaissance to investigate the presence of American aircraft. In fact, Gaddafi initially claimed that the US had shot down two "unarmed" reconnaissance aircraft over international waters. He further claimed that the encounter had been an act of "terrorism" and requested an emergency meeting of the UN Security Council. Gaddafi wanted the US condemned for its actions.

During an impassioned speech, Libya's envoy to the United Nations, Ali Sunni Muntasser, stated "'I am saying to you they were unarmed. They were reconnaissance planes, and everyone knows reconnaissance planes are not planes of aggression or attack."

The evidence, however, suggested otherwise.

Aerial photographs from the F-14s' on-board cameras clearly showed the lead MiG-23 armed with AA-7 Apex and AA-8 Aphid missiles. Moreover, the on-board video and audio recordings revealed that the American pilots made multiple attempts to evade the Libyan MiGs. The aggressive pursuit from the MiGs, therefore, sent a clear signal to the F-14 pilots that the Libyans had hostile intent. The outgoing Secretary of Defense, Frank C. Carlucci, further defended the American pilots, saying: "I don't think they fired too early. If anything, they fired too late…I thought they had every right to fire [their missiles] a mile earlier."

As the debate waxed and waned into the 1990s, different theories arose regarding the intent of the Libyan pilots. One such theory stated that the MiG-23s lost communication with their ground radar station, resulting in an accidental merging with the F-14s. Three months after the incident, it was revealed that the MiG pilots had never turned on their radars. The Libyan government focused on this critical detail, as the MiG-23's onboard radar was needed to guide the Apex missile. US House Armed Services Committee Chairman, Les Aspin, opined that the turns made by the Libyan MiGs were too slight to be deemed "hostile." Nevertheless, Aspin defended the Tomcat pilots—stating that Libya had a history of firing first and that the MiGs' continued acceleration and pursuit could not be ignored. Indeed, the Libyans had visual contact on the F-14s for most of the encounter. Prudence and common sense should have persuaded the Libyan MiGs not to pursue the F-14s, but the enemy pilots nevertheless continued vectoring towards the Tomcats. Even if their angle of approach didn't meet the conventional notions for "hostile" intent, the MiGs' aggressive speed and deliberate "jinking" maneuvers were enough to establish that the Libyans were not engaging in a peaceful intercept. Although the US confirmed that both Libyan pilots had ejected, it remains unknown whether these pilots were ultimately recovered from the sea.

By 1992, public discussion of the incident had largely subsided. In the years that followed, Gaddafi dialed down his rhetoric and made diplomatic strides to "mend fences" with the international community. More to the point, Gaddafi had to accept the realization that his military posed no viable threat to the West.

Today, the airframes for both *Gypsy 207* and *Gypsy 202* are on display. The former *Gypsy 207* (Bureau Number: 159610) resides at the Udvar-Hazy Center near Dulles International Airport in Virginia. The former *Gypsy 202* (Bureau Number: 159437) rests at Davis-Monthan Air Force Base in Arizona—home to the famous "aircraft boneyard."

Desert Storm

In the summer of 1990, mankind stood on the brink of a new era. Gone were the days of the Cold War—the Iron Curtain had fallen and the once-mighty Soviet Union lay on its deathbed. After nearly fifty years of ideological struggle, the United States stood as the world's lone superpower. But as Communism disappeared from Eastern Europe, and America reaped the benefits of her "peace dividend," a new conflict loomed on the horizon.

On the morning of August 2, 1990, Iraqi forces under the command of Saddam Hussein invaded the tiny emirate of Kuwait. Within hours, the Kuwaiti defenses collapsed under the onslaught of the Iraqi Army. The invasion drew fierce condemnation from

A lone F-14 flies over the still-burning oil wells in Kuwait, set afire by the retreating Iraqi ground forces, 1991. (US Navy)

An F-14B Tomcat from Squadron VF-74 "Be-Devilers" rolls down Catapult 2 aboard the USS *Saratoga* during Operation Desert Storm, January 1991. With the intent of driving Iraqi forces from Kuwait, the US-led coalition launched a 30-day air campaign to weaken the forces of Saddam Hussein. The aerial bombardment was followed by a 100-hour ground war, after which the Iraqi Army surrendered. (US Navy)

the international community and prompted the United Nations to demand Saddam's withdrawal. Undeterred by the rhetoric, the Iraqi dictator massed his forces along the Saudi Arabian border and dared the world to stop him.

Saddam was certain that his army—the fourth-largest in the world and equipped with the latest in Soviet armor—would make short order of any rescue force that came to liberate Kuwait. He wagered that the Americans would lead a military response against Iraq but, as he famously quipped, America was "a society that cannot accept 10,000 dead in one battle." Indeed, the memories of Vietnam were as galvanizing to Saddam Hussein as they were disheartening to the American public. He was confident that after the Americans had suffered a few thousand casualties, they would sue for peace on Iraq's terms. But for as tough as Saddam's army sounded, his air force was primitive by NATO standards. Although the Iraqi Air Force had the vaunted MiG-25 and MiG-29, the Iraqis had no viable air defense grid—a mistake that would cost them dearly in the opening days of the air campaign.

Saddam Hussein rose to power in 1968 following the Ba'ath Party revolution. However, as he ascended to the presidency, Saddam ruled Iraq with a brand of brutality reminiscent of Hitler and Stalin. Consolidating his power into a dictatorship, he seemed poised for a long, prosperous rule of Iraq…until his fortunes changed in the wake of the Iranian Revolution.

Fearful that the Ayatollah's rhetoric would influence Iraq's Shiite majority, Saddam preemptively invaded Iran on September 22, 1980. The ensuing Iran-Iraq War lasted eight years and ended in a bloody stalemate that claimed more than 300,000 Iraqi dead. Aside from the untold cost in human suffering, the conflict left Saddam straddled with a multi-billion-dollar war debt, most of which had been financed by Kuwait. Prior to the war, Iraq had almost no foreign debt and more than $35 billion in cash reserves. By 1989, however, Iraq had spent nearly $60 billion in arms purchases alone. But rather than pay his debt to the Kuwaiti government, the "Butcher of Baghdad" simply invaded his neighbor to the south. To justify the invasion, Saddam reignited the long-standing border dispute between the two countries. He also made false allegations that the Kuwaitis had been slant-drilling Iraqi oil and that they were deliberately trying to keep the price of oil low by producing beyond OPEC quotas. Kuwait held ten percent of the world's oil reserves and generated 97 billion barrels of crude each year. Thus, Saddam reasoned that if he could not repay his debt, he would simply annex the tiny emirate and take over its petroleum industry.

Thus, on the morning of August 2, more than 100,000 Iraqi troops and several hundred Iraqi tanks stormed across the border, the spearhead of an eighty-mile blitzkrieg into Kuwait City. Encountering only piecemeal resistance, Iraqi tanks thundered into the

Flying from VF-33, this Tomcat returns to the carrier deck after completing another aerial patrol in support of Operation Desert Shield, December 1990. "Desert Shield" referred to the initial deployment of coalition forces to the Persian Gulf, acting as a deterrent to Saddam Hussein, lest he try to invade the Kingdom of Saud. (US Navy)

A pair of F-14s from VF-32 on a Combat Air Patrol during Desert Storm. The F-14 in the background is armed with the AIM-9 Sidewinder missile (on the outer portion of the wing), the AIM-7 Sparrow missile (inner portion), and the AIM-54 Phoenix missile (beneath the fuselage). At the start of the Persian Gulf War, the F-14 was the only in-service Navy fighter with a prior air-to-air victory. (US Navy)

heart of the Kuwaiti capital, assaulting the city's central bank and carrying off with its wealth. A coordinated air-ground attack decimated the Dasman Palace, home to Kuwait's ruler Emir Jabel al-Amhad al-Sabar. The emir and a few members of his staff barely escaped with their lives as they fled Kuwait by helicopter. The last transmission made over the state-run radio network was an appeal for help.

The United Nations responded with their normal variety of condemnations. Economic and military sanctions soon followed while President George HW Bush authorized the first US deployments to the region. Within days, the aircraft carriers *Saratoga*, *Independence*, and *Eisenhower* were steaming towards the Persian Gulf while coalition air squadrons began pouring into Saudi Arabia by the hundreds. The first wave of deployments became known as "Operation Desert Shield"—a deterrent against Saddam Hussein lest he try to invade the Kingdom of Saud.

When Iraqi forces invaded Kuwait, US naval air forces were already poised to strike. In August 1990, the two closest carrier groups to the Persian Gulf were the ones led by the USS *Independence*, currently on maneuvers in the Indian Ocean, and the *Eisenhower*, then located in the central Mediterranean Sea. Within days of the Iraqi invasion, the *Independence* arrived in the Arabian Sea, well within striking distance of Saddam's occupation force. The *Eisenhower*, meanwhile, departed the Mediterranean through the Suez Canal, settling into the Red Sea by August 8. Within the next few months, *six* more carrier groups had arrived in the region. By September, the *Saratoga* and *John F.*

A Squadron VF-33 F-14A Tomcat aircraft flies a Combat Air Patrol (CAP) during Desert Storm. Despite the Tomcat's versatility and prior combat record, the plane was relegated largely to a support role—flying aerial reconnaissance, strike escort, and uneventful CAPs. (US Navy)

Kennedy had arrived in the Red Sea, awaiting orders to strike targets in western Iraq. Meanwhile, on the other side of the Arabian Peninsula, the carriers *Theodore Roosevelt, America, Ranger,* and *Midway* arrived in the Persian Gulf, poised to engage targets in eastern Iraq and Kuwait proper.

This consolidated naval force carried ten F-14 squadrons and twelve F/A-18 strike fighter squadrons. Alongside their Air Force and Marine Corps counterparts, a total of ninety-nine F-14 Tomcats participated in the campaign to liberate Kuwait. These Tomcats were part of the nearly 700 combat aircraft facilitating the Allied war effort. All told, it was the largest combined air force since World War II.

In November 1990, as coalition forces poured into Saudi Arabia, the UN passed Resolution 678. The resolution, for what it was worth, gave Saddam Hussein a deadline of January 15 to withdraw his forces, or face military action. Still, the Iraqi dictator showed no signs of backing down.

Achieving air superiority would be critical to the outcome of the war, but air power alone wouldn't bring Saddam to heel. In fact, General H. Norman Schwarzkopf, the Commander-in-Chief of UN forces in the Gulf, later noted that: "Colin Powell and I understood very early on that a strategic-bombing campaign in and of itself had never won a war and had never forced anybody to do anything if they wanted to sit it out." Thus, UN forces elected to use air power within an overlapping, four-phase strategy:

Phase 1: Destruction of Iraqi Communication, Command, and Control Nodes.

Phase 2: Air Defense Suppression

Phase 3: Battlefield Preparation

Phase 4: Ground Offensive with Air Support

During Phase 1, Allied aircraft would target key Iraqi telecommunications and command networks. A combination of Tomahawk missiles (fired from off-shore naval batteries) and precision-guided weapons (launched from strategic bombers and attack aircraft) would destroy the Iraqis' "eyes and ears" throughout the battlespace. The second phase would begin with day-and-night aerial strikes on Iraqi airfields and critical air defense sites. During this phase, the Allies would use every aircraft at their disposal—F-14 Tomcats; F-15 Eagles; F-111 Aardvarks; F-117 Nighthawks; F-4G Wild Weasels; A-6 Intruders; and the vaunted B-52 heavy bombers. Phase 3 would likewise target Iraqi infrastructure and include traditional "carpet bombing" with non-precision, kinetic energy bombs. During Phase 4, coalition ground forces would begin their assault into Iraqi territory, supported by attack aircraft including A-6 Intruder and the "tank busting" A-10 Warthog.

On the morning of January 15, 1991, coalition forces awoke to the news that Saddam Hussein had reached his deadline—and had made no effort to withdraw from Kuwait. The next day, President Bush announced the start of the military campaign to eject the

As seen from the cockpit of one of the aircraft, four Tomcats from Squadron VF-41 vector into Iraqi airspace in support of a strike mission on February 2, 1991. (US Navy)

A lone Tomcat from Squadron VF-103 prepares to re-fuel from a US Air Force aerial tanker on February 4, 1991. (US Air Force)

Iraqis from the war-torn emirate.

Operation Desert Shield had just become Operation *Desert Storm.*

On January 17, at 2:38 AM, Baghdad time, the first wave of the coalition's air campaign destroyed Iraqi radar sites near the Saudi border. For the next five weeks, coalition air forces pounded away at key targets within Iraq and Kuwait.

Interestingly, of the American aircraft that served in Desert Storm, the F-14 was the only in-service fighter with a previous air-to-air kill. Due to the Tomcats' flexibility and durability, the Navy deployed its F-14 squadrons aboard all but one of the carriers sent to the region—the USS *Midway.* Due to its smaller girth, the *Midway* carried three squadrons of F/A-18s and two A-6 Intruder squadrons. The carriers that did accommodate the F-14 featured a familiar cast of highly-decorated squadrons. The USS *John F. Kennedy,* for example, carried Squadrons VF-14 "Tophatters" and VF-32 "The Fighting Swordsmen", the latter of which had distinguished themselves against the Libyan MiGs during the second Gulf of Sidra Incident in 1989. Aboard the USS *Saratoga* were Squadrons VF-74 "Be-Devilers" and VF-103 "Sluggers," both of whom had flown interference during the *Achille Lauro* Incident of 1985. Squadron VF-74 had also distinguished itself during Operation El Dorado Canyon. The USS *America,* meanwhile, delivered Squadrons VF-33 "Starfighters" and VF-102 "Diamondbacks." Aboard the USS *Ranger,* Squadrons VF-1 "Wolfpack" and VF-2 "Bounty Hunters," the inaugural F-14 squadrons, prepared for action. Finally, on the flight decks of the USS *Theodore Roosevelt,* Squadron VF-41 "Black Aces," the heroes of the first Gulf of Sidra Incident in 1981, and Squadron VF-84, the revered "Jolly Rogers," readied themselves for combat.

From the outset of Desert Storm, many assumed that the F-14 would be a deciding

The underside view of an F-14 from Squadron VF-33 as it returns to the USS *America* following an escort mission during Desert Storm. This Tomcat carries the normal variety of mission ordnance: AIM-9 Sidewinders, AIM-7 Sparrows, and AIM-54 Phoenix missiles. February 1991. (US Navy)

factor in the air campaign. And while the Tomcat certainly played a critical role, the F-14 found itself relegated mostly to surveillance and escort missions. Unfortunately for the Tomcat, the Air Force's F-15 Eagle took much of the glory in the realm of air-to-air combat. According to Commander Doug Denneny, who served as a Tomcat RIO with Squadron VF-14: "There was a lot of parochialism as to where the F-14 and F-15 fighter CAPs [Combat Air Patrols] were placed. The Eagles got the kills because it was the USAF's E-3 AWACS [Airborne Warning and Control System planes] that were running the show up north. They would even call Navy guys off and then bring in Eagles for easy pickings."

In a similar vein, Rick Morgan, who served as an EA-6B Prowler crewman with Squadron VAQ-141 "Shadowhawks," in Desert Storm, recalled the frustration felt by the F-14 pilots:

> "In CVW-8 [Carrier Air Wing 8 aboard the *Roosevelt*] we had two very good Tomcat squadrons, VF-84 and VF-41. They all thought—and probably reasonably so—that there would be more air-to-air action than they saw. Very soon it became apparent that MiG killing…was probably not going to happen, so flying TARPS missions became critical, as well as the easiest path to a Strike-Flight Air Medal for the VF [fighter squadron] guys.

Why so few kills? Word was the USAF (who wrote the Air Tasking Order) was taking the most lucrative CAP locations for their own F-15s and the F-14s just didn't have the opportunity. There was another story going around, apparently with some truth, that the Iraqi RWR [Radar Warning Receiver] systems were tuned for the AN/AWG-9 since it was the biggest threat system their arch enemies, the Iranians, had. As the story went, every time their gear picked up an AN/AWG-9 from a Navy Tomcat, they'd run the other way—and usually right into a group of waiting USAF Eagles.

We had another day when I saw an F-14 pilot throw his helmet across our intel center after a flight. He'd been on a North Gulf CAP and saw at least one Mirage F-1 underneath him. As I recall the story, he rolled in and was ready to shoot when the E-2 told him to hold fire as 'it's friendly.' He followed instructions and didn't pull the trigger, but came back in a lather because he was convinced it was Iraqi. We later found out it was actually a Qatari Air Force bird, supposedly on the first day they'd flown in the war—except nobody had told us of their participation! Navy discipline and a sharp E-2 crew had paid off and kept a certain 'blue-on-blue' [fratricide] from occurring."

Still, the frustrations over the fleeting MiGs were echoed by other crewmen. Dave Parsons, who served as a Tomcat RIO with Squadron VF-32, recalled that these Iraqi MiGs "wouldn't go anywhere near an F-14." According to Parsons, this was the main reason why the F-14 did not score any kills against fixed-wing aircraft. "It was obvious

F-14s from VF-33, VF-84, and VF-14 refuel from an Air Force KC-10A aerial tanker. Throughout much of Desert Storm, American Tomcats had to rely on Air Force assets for fuel and battlespace directions. Given the F-14s' comparative shortage of air-to-air combat during the Gulf War, many within the naval aviation community accused the Air Force AWACS of directing their own F-15s onto the best targets while largely ignoring the F-14s. (US Navy)

that the Iraqis did not want to fight," he continued, "and they were running from us."

All told, the F-14s' lack of aerial combat had been the result of the Navy's failure to properly integrate the carrier air wings as part of a joint air command. The F-14s also lacked the most up-to-date "Identification Friend or Foe" (IFF) equipment found aboard the F-15 Eagle. This meant that the F-14s were unable to decipher the Rules of Engagement criteria and thus required clearance from Air Force AWACS to engage hostile targets.

Although the Tomcats' missions did not have the panache of the F-15 Eagles', the Tomcats' Tactical Airborne Reconnaissance Pod System (TARPS) made it an aircraft without equal in the skies over Iraq. Indeed, the TARPS were critical in locating mobile Scud sites and provided target information for fellow aircraft. For every Combat Air Patrol, the F-14 normally flew with a complement of two AIM-54C Phoenix missiles, four AIM-7F Sparrows, and a pair of AIM-9 Sidewinders. For TARP-specific missions, however, the Sparrow missiles were removed and subsequently replaced with a chaff adaptor and the AN/ALQ-167 jamming pod.

It was during a strike escort mission, however, that the Navy lost its only F-14 in combat. On January 21, 1991, merely four days into the air campaign, Lieutenant Devon Jones and his RIO, Lieutenant Lawrence Slade, from Squadron VF-103, took off from the flight decks of the USS *Saratoga*. Flying an F-14 call-signed *Slate 46* (Bureau Number 161430), Jones and Slade flew near Baghdad and the Al-Asad airbase.

"We had an early morning strike," Jones recalled, "50 miles into central Iraq," at just after 6:00 AM, local time. To this point, most of the Tomcats in the region were conducting strike escort missions. On average, these escort missions were three hours in

Preceded by its shadow, this F-14 from VF-41 "Black Aces," passes over western Saudi Arabia, 1991. (US Navy)

length and required at least one aerial refueling. "Our particular mission was to escort a single EA-6B with HARMS [High-speed Anti-radiation Missile]. Our Prowler was to go to 45 miles and take a pre-briefed HARM shot, pressing in from a west-to-east axis. At 30 miles, on the same axis, he would look for a target-of-opportunity shot. If there wasn't anything there, we'd turn around and egress."

It was a damp and cloudy night, less-than-ideal conditions for combat aviation but, as Jones noted, "I felt comfortable above the clouds." As *Slate 46* and their attendant Prowler approached the 45-mile mark, the EA-6B fired its HARM air-to-ground missile. Both aircraft were flying between 26,000 and 30,000 feet and, sensing no secondary targets, both aircraft prepared to egress. As *Slate 46* vectored to the left, however, Jones detected a surface-to-air missile rising from the clouds. "My RIO [Slade] saw it, too. It turned out to be an old SA-2, like the ones used in Vietnam."

Instinctively, Jones took his F-14 into evasive action.

"I added power, rolled into the SAM…to give the missile tracking problems." Sadly, his evasive maneuver wasn't fast enough. As Jones rolled the Tomcat downward, the missile tracked him, coming up towards the tail of *Slate 46*, detonating with a flash of blinding light. The Tomcat shuddered violently, but kept rolling to the right. Unbeknownst to Jones and Slade, the aircraft's tail had just been severed.

"The impact ripped my mask off," Jones recalled, "which was a big distraction and very frustrating because now we were going down and the mask was flopping all around." Struggling to re-apply his oxygen mask, Jones and his RIO were being thrashed around the cockpit as their F-14 went into a flat spin. "It was obvious that I was not going to recover the aircraft, so I pulled the [ejection] handle just as my RIO was starting to go for the handle himself." With the F-14 careening towards the desert floor, and the altimeter unable to track their descent, Slade and Jones ejected at nearly 10,000 feet.

"I was conscious through the entire ejection," said Jones, "because I remember the blast and the opening shock." Both men ejected safely, but their parachutes meandered off in different directions. As Jones drifted down towards the desert floor, he saw his RIO's parachute deploy from a distance of approximately 500 feet. "We lost sight of each other as we disappeared through the clouds." Come what may, Jones was confident that he and Slade would emerge from the debacle unscathed.

Meanwhile, their wingman aboard the EA-6B had seen the F-14 go down, and made the obligatory distress call. Slade had likewise made a distress call from his PRC-112 radio during the parachute descent. Now, the carrier group knew that one of its own had been shot down. Soon, all coalition aircraft in the area would be advised of the same. The more pressing matter for the downed crew of *Slate 46*, however, was the Iraqi ground forces.

As Jones drifted onto the ground, he took stock of the situation. "Now, reality finally hit me," he said. "I was down on the ground, inside Iraq. I could see my Tomcat's crash site and the ball of flames." Knowing that the Iraqis would not take kindly to an American POW, Jones hastily departed the scene, recalling his training from the Survival, Evasion, Resistance, and Escape (SERE) Course. As he regained his bearings, he made a distress call, signaling that he was still alive and, from what he could deduce, his RIO had likewise survived the crash. Meanwhile, Jones headed east, trying to reach Slade on his radio.

No such luck.

At about 9:00 AM, Jones spied something "blue and cylindrical," in his peripheral vision. From what he could deduce, the object appeared to be two miles from his current location and resembled a small automobile. As he approached it, however, he realized it was some sort of water tank, approximately 20 feet long. With nothing more than his survival knife, Jones began digging a hole in the dirt. "I dug for an hour," he said, "and ended up with a hole four feet long and three feet deep. My hands were blistered and bloodied but it was a pretty good-sized hole." Crawling into his new hiding spot, Jones took off as much of his flight gear as he could. "I laid on my radio and tried to get comfortable."

Throughout the day, Jones heard the sound of aircraft flying overhead, but couldn't tell if the planes were American or Iraqi.

Later that morning, however, he heard the sound of an approaching truck.

Peering out from his spider hole, Jones saw a blue, stake-bed truck, approaching the water tank. "My heart was pounding," he said. Jones could tell from its appearance that the truck was a farming vehicle, but had no idea if its occupants were civilian or military. He was relieved, however, when he saw two plain-clothes Iraqi farmers exit the cab. Maintaining his silence, Jones hunkered down in his hole while the two Iraqis inspected the tank, presumably looking for water or fuel. After three minutes, and seeing that the tank was empty, the Iraqi farmers quickly departed the scene.

Shortly after 12:00 noon, Jones tried again to raise someone on the radio. "I was still trying to contact my RIO," he said. Little did he know, however, that Slade had already been captured. Suddenly, through the crackling static of his radio, Jones heard American voices.

"*Slate 46*, how do you read?"

To his surprise, the anonymous voice on the other end had identified him by his callsign. "That was the first time that I knew anyone even knew my callsign, or that there had been an ongoing SAR [Search and Rescue] effort." Jones was elated, but wondered to whom the anonymous voice belonged. A SEAL Team? Air Force Para-rescue?

"Look to your south," the voice continued, "I'll pickle a flare. I'm at 18,000 feet."

Instantly, Jones knew the voice belonged to an aviator, and complied with the instruction to keep his eyes on the southern horizon.

"Ok, now I'll come down to where you can see me," the voice continued.

Jones brimmed with delight as he saw an A-10 Warthog descend from the clouds—"a 'Sandy', like those guys in Vietnam, trained in combat SAR." Jones directed the A-10 onto his location, and although the Warthog pilot did not see Jones, the plane flew a mere 100 feet above the water tank and relayed the location to an Air Force heliborne rescue squad.

As the helicopters scrambled to Jones's location, however, they detected a flight of Iraqi MiGs being vectored to intercept. But luckily for the rescue squad, a nearby flight of F-15s had just picked up the same signal from the incoming MiGs. "As soon as the F-15s got their vectors," Jones recalled, "the MiGs ran away." The A-10s then escorted the helicopters to Jones' location.

By now, Jones could hear the faint staccato of the incoming rotor blades. But, as Jones admitted, he had made a critical mistake when identifying his location to the rescue squad. When asked for his location relative to the crash site, Jones replied that he was

In what became a common sight during the later stages (and aftermath) of the Gulf War, Kuwaiti oil wells burn uncontrollably. Having been set ablaze by retreating Iraqi forces, coalition ground crews worked feverishly to extinguish the flames. Meanwhile, F-14s like this one from VF-84 conducted fly-overs to assess the damage. (US Navy)

about ten miles north of the wreckage, but added that he was in the vicinity of the blue tank. "The Iraqis must have been listening to our transmissions," he said, "and, of course, they must have known where the tank was." Indeed, moments later, an Iraqi Army truck appeared over the southern horizon—barreling straight towards Jones and the landmark blue tank. "I think we all saw it at the same time," said Jones, because the A-10 came on the radio with: "We've got a fast mover on the dirt road."

Admittedly, Jones was panicking, but his panic turned to relief when he saw the 30mm guns from the A-10s make short work of the Iraqi vehicle. Indeed, after two strafing runs, the A-10s had left nothing but flames and dust of the Iraqi troop truck. By the time the Iraqi truck plodded to a fiery halt, it was barely 100 yards from Jones's hiding spot. "I guess the Iraqis had finally figured out where I was through all our radio talk."

The lead helicopter touched down about twenty yards from Jones's spider hole. "One of the special forces guys jumped out and waved me on," he recalled. "I jumped in and off we went, 140 miles to go at 140 knots." He had spent eight hours behind enemy lines. Returning to his squadron, Jones was eternally grateful to the Air Force comrades who had risked their lives to save his own. "Big spines on these guys, I'll tell you, being 150 miles into enemy territory during the day."

Lieutenant Slade, however, hadn't been so lucky.

Touching down on the desert floor, Slade knew that the crash site would draw attention from nearby ground forces. "I needed to get as far away from the crash site as possible," he said. "I estimated I landed five to 10 miles away from the plane, because of the winds."

Over the next two and half hours, he traversed the Iraqi desert on foot, attempting new radio calls to Jones and any nearby coalition unit.

No reply came.

With no luck finding Jones, or establishing radio contact with him, Slade took pause to study his surroundings. "The terrain was very dry and flat," he said, "and I came to a small, round knoll. Dawn was breaking and I needed to find some place to hide. I tried to use my survival knife to dig in but the land was too hard, too rocky. So, I just dusted myself up to try to blend in a little."

At approximately 10:30 that morning, however, Slade was intercepted by a small white Datsun pickup truck. Driven by two Iraqi men—one carrying a 12-gauge shotgun; the other carrying an AK-47—Slade noted that the both the truck and its drivers seemed out of place.

Both men spoke English, but their appearance seemed off.

The man with the AK-47 was dressed in a shabby, green Iraqi uniform that looked more like a thrift store find. The man with the shotgun, however, was obviously a Bedouin. Despite their mismatched appearance, the two men ordered Slade to strip off his flight gear.

Seeing that he was outgunned, Slade begrudgingly complied.

According to Slade, however, these Iraqi men were polite and later fed him. Although they were armed, Slade noticed that the pair didn't seem to carry themselves like soldiers. "Maybe they were just friends driving around." Thus, he assumed that his capture "was probably bad luck because I don't think they were looking for me; they were just driving by." The men asked Slade if he wanted to go to Saudi Arabia or Baghdad. Slade responded "Saudi Arabia," but after a three-and-a-half-hour drive, the truck pulled into an army camp that he knew was in Baghdad.

Slade, 26 years old at the time, was handcuffed and blindfolded, then moved through six different camps over the course of the day. "My captors would throw me in the truck and drive me to the different places, usually 45 minutes apart," he recalled. "They'd take me out and ask me questions, very haphazardly, nothing very organized. It was clear these were not real interrogations. I was obviously a subject of interest and was probably working my way up to the main camp." Through this process, Slade was pushed, kicked, cursed, and yelled at, sometimes in English, with phrases like "You kill our children!"

"I spent that night in Baghdad, beginning three days of hardcore interrogation," he said. "Then I was shuttled off to a prison, the first one, actually. At that point, they took my blindfold off, after three days. I was in a cell by myself, but I could communicate with other prisoners." Over the three-day interrogation, he evaded answering questions to the best of his ability. Many times, he purposely gave answers that were, in his own words, "complete garbage."

Eleven days after his capture, Slade and his fellow POWs were moved to another prison inside Baghdad where, from what he could deduce, his handlers were Ba'ath Party civilians. "We stayed in the jail until the end of February, then moved to another army prison. Our care was much better there. The bombing had stopped by then, and we began to think that maybe we could see the end of it all."

Throughout his time as a POW, Slade endured a total of six interrogations—all of which had him double-blindfolded and beaten with his hands tied behind his back. In

F-14 Tomcats from VF-114 "Aardvarks," conduct fly-over assessments of the burning oil fields in Kuwait. Although VF-114 was not directly involved in the Gulf War, it deployed to the Persian Gulf soon thereafter to assist in the post-war efforts. It would be the squadron's last deployment—VF-114 was disestablished on April 30, 1993. (US Navy)

While returning to the USS *Eisenhower*, an F-14 Tomcat from VF-143 surveys the damage from the Iraqis' "scorched-earth" policy, 1991. (US Navy)

fact, many of his interrogations followed a cyclical pattern: tied, blindfolded, and beaten even when he gave a seemingly satisfactory response. "It was an exercise in patience for me," he said, "taking things one day at a time." He later admitted that he "had no expectation of living through the experience," but Slade was nevertheless held as a POW for forty-three days. The interrogations and beatings continued throughout his captivity, including a severe incident in late February 1991 when his handlers threw him against a wall so hard that it broke his seventh vertebra.

Slade's fellow POWs at the various prisons included a couple of British Tornado crews, an A-6 crew, and a Marine OV-10 crew. All were kept under the highest scrutiny of the Iraqi Army, and the POWs themselves became a media sensation when the Iraqi government broadcast videotapes of their captivity.

On March 4, 1991, four days after the end of Operation Desert Storm, Slade and his captured comrades were turned over to the American Red Cross. Slade, however, had suffered irreparable damage at the hands of his captors. After forty days of being served nothing more than "oily-water" soup, he had lost more than forty pounds, suffering damage to his internal organs. Evacuating from the Middle East, he flew to Bethesda Naval Hospital, where he spent the next few weeks in recovery. On March 21, 1991, Slade returned home to Virginia Beach, where a crowd of more than 5,000 supporters (and a Navy band) was there to welcome him. For his perseverance, emotional stamina, and conduct under fire, Lieutenant Slade received the Purple Heart and the Prisoner of War Medal.

Navigating its way through the fire and smoke of the oil fields, this F-14 from Squadron VF-211 returns to its carrier. (US Navy)

A few weeks after Jones and Slade tragically lost their Tomcat to enemy fire, Squadron VF-1 earned the distinction of achieving the F-14's first (and only) air-to-air victory of Desert Storm. Indeed, the Tomcat's sole aerial victory of the war occurred on February 6, 1991. The engagement was noteworthy because the target was a *helicopter*—the first rotary aircraft ever shot down by an American crew in combat.

That morning, pilot Lieutenant Stuart "Meat" Broce, and his RIO, Commander Ron "Bongo" McElraft, catapulted from the flight decks of the USS *Ranger*, flying the F-14 call-signed *Wichita 103* (Bureau Number 162603) providing air cover for an EA-6B Prowler sent on a jamming mission in support of another air strike on Kuwait.

But *Wichita 103* wasn't alone that day, as another F-14 from Squadron VF-1, piloted by Lieutenant Scott "Ash" Malynn and his RIO, Lieutenant Dan "Zymby" Zimberoff, joined them as their wingman. *Wichita 103* took the lead toward the rendezvous point but, along the way, the pair of F-14s received new orders to proceed to another Combat Air Patrol station to observe any enemy activity. The site of this Combat Air Patrol was farther north, beyond where most coalition aircraft had flown, except for the F-15 Eagles. Moreover, the F-15s had previously engaged Iraqi MiGs in this patrol sector. Thus, while heading into this area of known conflict, the Tomcat crews reviewed their ammunition loads.

Each had four AIM-9 Sidewinder and four AIM-7 Sparrow missiles.

Soon after arrival at their destination, the Tomcats received new orders to engage. As they were now beyond the range of their normal E-2 Hawkeyes, the F-14s began taking directions from the Air Force E-3 AWACS.

"Wolfpack, engage bandit, vector 210-36, angels low, nose on!"

Acknowledging the AWACS's call, the Tomcats turned to a heading of 210 degrees and would engage the Iraqi aircraft at 36 miles. According to the AWAC's transmission, both Tomcats were also expecting the bandit to be at a lower altitude, heading straight for them. As Broce steered his Tomcat onto the proper heading, Commander McElraft confirmed *Wichita 103's* clearance to fire.

The AWACS responded: "Affirmative! Cleared hot, weapons free!"

Broce then flipped the master arm switch to 'ON' and announced "Recorder on!" to properly document the engagement. As Broce recalled: "I wanted it recorded on our onboard HUD camera/voice recorder, and either debriefed back at the boat, or pulled from the wreckage and reviewed."

Along the way, the E-3 AWACS updated Broce and his wingman with new bearing and range information. Near the proper coordinates, Broce had just leveled *Wichita 103* at 3,000 feet when RIO McElraft called out:

"Come left! Helicopter!"

Broce immediately pulled a 7g turn and, after shaking off the g-force, he visually spotted a Soviet-built Mi-8 helicopter, two miles out. This particular variant of the Mi-8 was an armed transport. Broce noted that the Mi-8 was going exceptionally fast for a helicopter and it appeared to be headed for a nearby village.

From his current angle, Lieutenant Broce knew that a Sparrow missile wouldn't suffice; thus, he prepped the AIM-9 Sidewinder, pitching the Tomcat's nose upward to align his shot. He was maneuvering and waiting for the heat seeker tone to announce when he had a lock on. Unfortunately, because *Wichita 103* was already at a dangerously low altitude, and moving closer to the ground every second, there wasn't much time to wait for the perfect shot.

Trying to get a tone on the helicopter, and quickly running out of altitude, "I let the nose drift a little behind the target on a hunch that there was enough of a heat signature for a lock, despite the lack of tone," he said. "The HUD's [Heads-Up Display] seeker head position indicator stayed superimposed on the helicopter as it drifted slightly from center. In a fraction of a second, I thought 'Well, that's as good as it'll get today, and I've got three more…*and* a bunch of bullets.' So I pulled the trigger."

Meanwhile, the F-14 was getting so low that McElraft, from his backseat, was beginning to panic. Unaware that Broce was trying to line up a missile shot, and seeing the ground getting dangerously closer to *Wichita 103*, McElraft yelled:

"Pull up! What the hell are you…"

But just then, his transmission was interrupted by Broce firing the Sidewinder missile. McElraft punctuated his transmission with a surprised and satisfied "Oh…," happily watching the Sidewinder slide off its rail.

It was the first Sidewinder that Broce had fired in combat, and the noise was such that it drowned out the sound of the engines. As the missile flew past the canopy, Broce hoped that there was enough of a heat signature for the missile to lock on. At first

Flight deck personnel use their MD-3A tow tractor to move an F-14 from Squadron VF-74 into position on the USS *Saratoga* during Desert Storm. January 1991. (US Navy)

glance, however, the missile appeared to be heading towards a nearby sand dune in front of the helicopter. Broce silently cursed to himself, thinking that his missile had "gone stupid" and that he would have to destroy the helicopter with his autocannons. Suddenly, however, the missile corrected itself, turning hard left and barreling straight into the starboard exhaust of the Mi-8. The fleeing helicopter exploded into what Broce described as a "bright yellow fireball," before its fiery carcass crashed onto the desert floor. The fireball sent pieces of the fuselage in every direction, and Broce had to pull up hard on *Wichita 103* to avoid the wreckage and debris.

McElraft then reported the downed helicopter to the Carrier Air Wing, but soon realized that there was no special code word to denote killing a rotary aircraft. It seemed that the naval aviation community hadn't considered the likelihood of an F-14 engaging a helicopter. Thus, when McElraft radioed confirmation of Broce's kill, he reported:

"Uh, splash one, uhhhh…helicopter!"

Wichita 103 patrolled for another six hours, refueling twice in the air. As night fell, Broce and McElraft, along with Malynn and Zimberoff, departed the CAP sector to the Gulf. "On the way out of Iraq," Broce recalled, "at AWACS request," we descended back through the weather to perform battle damage assessment on a very recently attacked strategic target. We stayed close together and broke out pretty low in the dusk…we literally flew among the burning remnants of the bombed-out facility. The scene was surreal; our night low-level lit by fires on the ground." Taking stock of the battle damage on the ground, *Wichita 103* passed its assessment back to the requesting AWACS before returning the USS *Ranger* later that night.

Unfortunately for Broce and McElraft, despite having called "Recorder on!," both crewmen had forgotten to insert a tape into the flight recorder, meaning that there had been no video footage of the altercation.

The remainder of Desert Storm was relatively uneventful for the F-14—a fact that angered many within the naval fighter community. Indeed, the F-14 pilots, and their advocates, believed that the Gulf War had been a perfect opportunity to demonstrate the Tomcat's versatility in a sustained, high-intensity conflict. For much of the war, however, the Tomcat had been relegated to a supporting role—largely due to the parochialism and organizational politics between the US Navy and Air Force. The F-14's viability in combat could have been highlighted through its air-to-ground capabilities, but the F/A-18 Hornet garnered most of the attention, and subsequent praise, in that regard.

Despite its somewhat diminished role, the F-14 nevertheless had a profound impact on the air war against Iraq. Indeed, the mere presence of a Tomcat was typically enough to discourage the Iraqi MiGs from engaging. Considering the havoc and devestation wreaked by the Ayatollah's F-14s during the Iran-Iraq War, one could hardly blame Iraqi pilots for likewise wanting to avoid American Tomcats.

As the air campaign lumbered into its second month, coalition ground forces began their assault into Iraq on February 24, 1991. Barely 100 hours after the start of the Allied invasion, however, the Iraqi Army was in full retreat and Saddam Hussein was desperate to sue for peace. Meanwhile, much of the Iraqi Air Force had been destroyed on the ground—and the few remaining planes in the air were becoming easy targets for coalition aircraft. On February 27, 1991, President Bush announced the official cease-fire. In their disastrous retreat, the Iraqis had fled Kuwait, leaving a devastated country in their wake. It would take a massive reconstruction effort to get the emirate back on its feet; but for now, the savagery of Iraq's occupation had ended. On March 3, 1991, General H. Norman Schwarzkopf met with several Iraqi generals in Safwan to discuss the terms of surrender.

For the F-14 Tomcat, however, the Gulf War was a missed opportunity to prove its worth in the face of the F-15, F-16, and its up-and-coming stablemate, the F/A-18 Hornet. Come what may during the 1990s, the F-14 would struggle to remain relevant in a post-Cold War military that favored lighter, leaner aircraft.

The Inter-war Years

Following the end of Operation Desert Storm, the United States realized that a military presence was still necessary in the Persian Gulf. A Shi'ite rebellion had erupted during the postwar chaos while the Iraqi Kurds (already a targeted minority under the Ba'athist regime) attempted to flee the heavy-handed rule of Saddam Hussein. Thus, to protect the ethnic Kurds in the north, and the Shi'ite Muslims in the south, the US created and enforced "No-Fly Zones" over northern and southern Iraq—patrolled by fighter jets flown primarily from Incirlik Air Base in Turkey. Citing UN Resolution 688, the United States mandated that no Iraqi military aircraft could enter the No-Fly

As seen from the cockpit of an F-14 from Squadron VF-41, two other Tomcats fly in formation to a rendezvous point on May 2, 1991 during Operation Provide Comfort I, the multinational effort to aid Kurdish refugees in southern Turkey and northern Iraq. (US Navy)

From the flight deck of the USS *Theodore Roosevelt*, an F-14 from Squadron VF-84 "Jolly Rogers" prepares to launch from the catapult in support of Operation Provide Comfort I, May 1991. (US Navy)

Zones. Any wandering aircraft found within the No-Fly Zones would, therefore, be engaged with hostile fire.

The first No-Fly Zone air patrols were dubbed "Operation Provide Comfort" and fell under the operational control of the United States European Command (EUCOM). As part of Provide Comfort's aerial task force, the F-14 returned to its standard roles of Combat Air Patrol, strike escort, and long-range reconnaissance. Unfortunately for the Tomcat crewmen, their F-14s were given little to do in the skies over postwar Iraq. To be certain, the F-14 was still a valuable asset, but military strategies of the 1990s were rapidly changing—and the need for a carrier-based interceptor was not as urgent as it once had been. Indeed, the skies were no longer filled with Soviet bombers to intercept or Libyan bandits to outmaneuver.

During that short period of Operation Provide Comfort (March - July 1991) the assigned F-14 squadrons flew hundreds of sorties—one of which was VF-84 "The Jolly Rogers," which flew 111 missions from the USS *Roosevelt*.

The F-14s continued to patrol the skies during subsequent operations in the Iraqi No-Fly Zones. Operation Provide Comfort II (July 1991 – December 1996) continued similar efforts as the first Provide Comfort. The primary objective was to curtail Saddam Hussein's ongoing aggression against the Kurds. Provide Comfort I and II were successful inasmuch as they facilitated the withdrawal of Iraqi troops from Kurdish territory in October 1991. Thereafter, the Kurds resumed their autonomy in northern Iraq.

Shortly after Provide Comfort I, and almost simultaneously with Provide Comfort II,

As the sun descends under the horizon, this F-14D Tomcat rests on the flight deck during a break in flight operations supporting Operation Southern Watch—the enforcement mission of the southern Iraqi "No-Fly Zone" below the 32d Parallel. (US Navy)

the US launched Operation Southern Watch—monitoring and controlling Iraqi airspace below the 32d Parallel. Southern Watch was a long-term initiative spanning from July 1992 until the subsequent invasion of Iraq in March 2003. During this time, Iraqi forces regularly fired upon American aircraft with surface-to-air missiles; all without much success. At first, American forces rarely responded to Iraq's anti-aircraft fire—focusing instead on completing their surveillance sorties. But when Saddam Hussein began pushing the limits and refusing to comply with UN demands (e.g. withdrawing surface-to-air missiles from select locations), Coalition air forces went on the offensive. Bombing missile sites and strategic locations, US and British warplanes engaged Iraqi ground targets with virtual impunity. For these missions, the F-14 had a recurring role as part of the Coalition strike packages. Likewise, the F-14 played a vital reconnaissance role via its onboard TARPS system—taking flight nearly every day to monitor Iraq's military activity.

These Tomcat missions over Iraq followed a standardized pattern. Indeed, 72 hours before takeoff, the shipboard mission planner received an outline of the Air Tasking Order (ATO). Over the next few days, the planning team would receive detailed mission parameters outlining target locations and disposition. For each mission, five Tomcats went aloft, but only four participated in the mission; the fifth Tomcat was an "aerial reserve," engaging targets only if needed. On the day of the mission, each pilot and his RIO attended a mission briefing, followed by a review of emergency in-flight procedures.

Against the background of the setting sun, this F-14D from VF-31 conducts another combat mission in support of Operation Southern Watch. Throughout the enforcement of the Iraqi No-Fly Zones, American F-14s distinguished themselves in their new contingency roles, particularly with regards to their flight endurance. Indeed, the Tomcat could stay aloft much longer than its up-and-coming stablemate, the F/A-18 Hornet. (US Navy)

After the last F-14 ascended from the flight deck, the Tomcat flight rendezvoused with additional aircraft, forming the entire mission strike package. Alongside this aerial armada was a fuel tanker, allowing each aircraft to replenish its fuel. Ironically, the F-14's fuel capacity gave it a decided advantage over its celebrated stablemate, the F/A-18 Hornet. On average, the F-14 Tomcat could stay aloft nearly twice as long as the Hornet. After replenishing their fuel and ensuring that all systems were operational, the strike packages departed for their intended targets.

Meanwhile, in the aftermath of Desert Storm, the Socialist Federal Republic of Yugoslavia began to fracture along ethnic and religious lines. A Communist state bordering the Adriatic Sea, Yugoslavia was the dominion of President Josip Broz Tito. Following Tito's death and the collapse of Communism in Eastern Europe, the ethnic and religious groups within Yugoslavia (including Serbs, Croats, et al) began jockeying for independence. These independence movements, however, soon devolved into a civil war—whereupon NATO and the United Nations intervened.

Beginning with Operation Sky Monitor in November 1992, followed by Operation Deny Flight in March 1993, American aircraft gradually increased their role in the skies over Yugoslavia. By the summer of 1993, US aircraft could fly fully-armed close air support missions in support of UN peacekeepers. According to Navy Lieutenant Todd Parker, who served as a RIO with Squadron VF-41:

"Carrier-borne F-14s were heavily involved in the policing of the UN-imposed 'No-Fly Zones,' and in providing air cover for transport aircraft conducting humanitarian relief operations. The Tomcats flew regular combat air patrols, looking for violations of the UN resolutions, and for unauthorized air activity by the combatants. NATO generally kept pairs of fighters airborne at two CAP stations for 24 hours per day, day-in, day-out. Serb helicopters were frequently found violating Bosnian airspace, but inevitably landed when challenged, resuming their activities once NATO fighters had left the area. USAF F-16s shot down four Serb Galebs [Yugoslavian-built fighter jets] in February 1994 but, generally, the rules of engagement were too tightly drawn to allow the F-14s to engage the enemy."

This quickly changed, however, in August 1994, when American planes were cleared to engage Serbian ground targets. This gave NATO pilots the chance to fly alongside many allies whom they had never seen before, all while sharpening their ground-attack skills. For the F-14, the war in Yugoslavia gave the D-variant "Bombcat" its time to shine. Parker continued:

"I had been a Radar Intercept Officer (RIO) in VF-41 for three years when we deployed in March 1995…on board the USS *Theodore Roosevelt*. This team had proved its lethality in the Gulf War, and those of us who had missed that opportunity were eagerly anticipating our shot. Things had been quiet in Bosnia for many months, primarily because of the winter weather, but we knew that the spring thaw usually

An F-14 roars past its attendant aviation boatswain's mate as it launches from the catapult of the USS *Independence* in support of Operation Southern Watch. February 22, 1998. (US Navy)

meant increased hostilities. From the Tomcat standpoint, we were especially excited about the chance to employ a truly multi-mission capable aircraft. In addition to our standard Combat Air Patrols...we would be flying Exercise Close Air Support (XCAS) and a newly-emerging Navy mission known as FAC(A) [Forward Air Control (Airborne)].

Once on station, we immediately began planning contingency operations, for clashes between the Bosnian Serbs and Bosnian Muslims were already occurring daily. Unfortunately, the first four missions that launched off the carrier—all CAS and FAC(A) missions—were as anti-climactic as the three months that followed.

In what became a routine drill for aircrew and planners alike, we would plan all night for a bombing mission we were certain would launch at first light, only to be shut down, sometimes literally, just before launch. Each event brought an intense 24-to 36-hour planning period, followed by the wait for the word to launch, which never came. As might be expected, after doing this many times over three months, morale can suffer, and it became increasingly difficult to muster motivation to plan a mission that we doubted would ever launch. But, plan we did."

Luckily, the squadron's collective fortunes were about to change. For on August 29, 1995, VF-41 successfully launched its first mission of the air campaign. Lieutenant Parker was happy that there had been no last-minute cancellation, but he still didn't think the mission would yield anything. Much to his surprise, however, the lead Tomcat returned to the flight deck at 2:00 AM with empty missile racks. As Parker remembered: "We could hardly contain our surprise and excitement. Finally, after so much hard work and

This F-14B, assigned to VF-102, is accompanied by an EA-6B Prowler aircraft during a mission in support of Operation Southern Watch, January 1998. Both aircraft flew from aboard the USS *George Washington*. (US Navy)

An F-14 taxies to the runway at Incirlik Air Base, Turkey on February 26, 2003 in support of Operation Northern Watch. As the successor to Operation Provide Comfort I and II, Northern Watch enforced the Northern No-Fly Zone and continued monitoring the welfare of Iraqi Kurds. (US Air Force)

so little return, we were getting the chance to prove ourselves."

Shortly thereafter, NATO's Combined Air Operations Center assigned the Tomcats to engage an ammunition depot in eastern Bosnia. However, due to the potential for collateral damage, this target could only be serviced by a laser-guided bomb. "At the time," said Parker, "we were not carrying the LANTIRN pod, which now provides Tomcats with a day or night, self-escort, self-lased precision guided munition (PGM) capability…we could employ any of the laser guided bombs as long as someone lased the target for us." Thus, these Tomcats had to go aloft with a pair of F/A-18 Hornets who would "buddy-lase" the target for the F-14 crew. "Two F-14s launched with the Hornet flight," Parker continued, "yet there was still the question of whether drop authority would really come for this unusual delivery tactic. Imagine the feeling of excitement when, two hours later, those same two Tomcats came back with their belly stations empty, except for the dangling wire that remains after the release of an electrically-fused weapon. The review of the FLIR tapes…proved that the planning and diligence had paid off: two bombs, two direct hits, and a history-making day for VF-41 and the Tomcat community at large."

Aside from being the first US Tomcat squadron to achieve an air-to-air victory (Gulf of Sidra, 1981), VF-41 now had the distinction of being the first Tomcat unit to deliver precision-guided bombs against hostile ground targets.

Two Tomcats from VF-103 fly over the Mediterranean Sea during their six-month deployment in support of Operation Southern Watch. US naval air squadrons continued supporting Operation Southern Watch after 9/11 and before the start of Operation Iraqi Freedom. In fact, before the 2003 invasion of Iraq, many F-14 squadrons simultaneously supported Southern Watch *and* Enduring Freedom. (US Navy)

Meanwhile, in the skies over Iraq, American Tomcats continued operating under the auspices of Southern Watch until December 16, 1998, when President Bill Clinton authorized Operation Desert Fox—a four-day bombardment of critical Iraqi targets. The stated goal of the operation was to eliminate any sites capable of manufacturing or delivering Weapons of Mass Destruction (WMD). Desert Fox was, at the time, the largest aerial strike against Iraq since the Gulf War.

Desert Fox also highlighted a few milestones in American military history. For instance, it was the first operation featuring female fighter pilots in combat. As a part of Carrier Air Wing 3 (CVW-3), Lieutenant Kendra Williams, Lieutenant Lyndsi Bates, and Lieutenant Carol Watts piloted their F/A-18C Hornets from the USS *Enterprise* for successful bombing missions. Desert Fox also debuted the Air Force's B-1B bomber, a supersonic variable sweep-wing heavy bomber. Moreover, Desert Fox gave the Tomcat an opportunity to expand its role as a bomb-dropping, ground assault aircraft.

Thus, with the carrier-based squadrons leading the way, the US Navy assumed the brunt of combat duty in the early days of Desert Fox. A strike leader assigned to Squadron VF-32 noted that the older F-14Bs were, "designed for a single cycle [single bomb runs] so as to achieve the element of surprise. Our F-14s were loaded with two 1,000lb GBU-16 [laser guided bombs], and our target was within the Baghdad city limits. Tomcats were assigned most of the hard targets because of the aircraft's LTS [LANTIRN Targeting

From the deck of the USS *Theodore Roosevelt*, this Tomcat prepares for a night launch on April 12, 1999, in support of Operation Allied Force—the NATO effort to expel Yugoslav forces from Kosovo. (US Navy)

System] capability - collateral damage was unacceptable. We found our targets and 'schwacked' them. To watch those buildings go away through the LTS cockpit display was impressive. We were opposed by ballistic-launched SAMs and AAA."

The F-14D Bombcats took off from the USS *Carl Vinson* on December 18, 1998. Venturing into the fray, their primary targets included WMD research and development sites, military installations, weapons depots, and Republican Guard centers. Due to the F-14's range of capabilities, it served as both an attack aircraft and escort-interceptor. As Commander Will Cooney noted after the operation, "The Tomcat's distinct size and power made it an intimidating foe to any enemy. With the big motors in the F-14B/D, its speed and power were very impressive. Coupled with size, large ordnance load, and long legs, the Tomcat could really reach out and touch the bad guys."

On December 19, 1998, the US terminated Operation Desert Fox, having successfully destroyed or damaged more than 30 Iraqi targets and having killed nearly 1,400 Republican Guard personnel. Throughout the operation, Tomcat squadrons flew more than 400 sorties. Squadron VF-32 alone dropped 111,054 pounds of ordnance—including 16 GBU-10s, 16 GBU-16s and at least twenty-six 2000-pound GBU-24 LGBs. These aerial sorties included the Tomcat's first use of the GBU-24 in combat and the first use of the F-14's newer Night Vision Devices (NVDs).

Following these hasty aerial bombardments in the Persian Gulf, the US Navy turned its attention once again to the Adriatic Sea. In March 1999, NATO began yet another military operation in the former Yugoslavia, this time in Kosovo. NATO—already having a foothold in the region due to its peacekeeping missions in Bosnia—was determined to drive the Yugoslavs from Kosovo on the grounds of humanitarian intervention. To affect these goals, the USS *Theodore Roosevelt*, and its attendant air squadrons, steamed towards the beleaguered Balkan Peninsula.

From aboard the flight decks of the *Roosevelt*, the Tomcats reprised their dual role of bomber and patrol interceptor. Over the course of three months, F-14 squadrons dropped nearly 800,000 pounds of laser-guided bombs and conventional munitions. Commander Ted Carter, a member of the Forward Air Control (Airborne) team, also known as "FAC(A)," explained the mission as such:

"We flew in sections, one aircraft serving as an escort for the other. Each F-14 usually carried four bombs, which we used for both striking a target ourselves or for marking a target for other strike aircraft. The FAC(A) is like a quarterback on a football team, seeking out and identifying targets, ushering strike aircraft to the scene, recommending the type of ordnance for a particular target, ensuring they recognized potential terrain hazards and providing them with run-in and recovery headings."

The mission in Kosovo ended on June 10, 1999—but the ongoing tensions with Iraq had not yet subsided. In January 1999, even before the campaign in Kosovo had begun, the Iraqi Air Force had begun challenging the No-Fly Zones. This time, the offenders were a pair of Iraqi MiG-23s. Two F-14Ds from Squadron VF-213 vectored to intercept. When the probing MiGs spotted the F-14s, however, the Iraqi pilots quickly fled the scene. However, a nearby Iraqi MiG-25 vectored towards the Tomcats' location. Picking up the newfound bandit on radar, the Tomcats fired two AIM-54 Phoenix missiles. The distance, however, was quite far and both missiles failed to track their target. Like his comrades had done moments earlier, this MiG-25 quickly departed.

This would not be the last time, however, that Iraqi pilots would challenge the No-Fly Zone. On September 9, 1999, an F-14 from Squadron VF-2 engaged two MiG-23s heading south into the No-Fly Zone from Al-Taqaddum Air Base, west of Baghdad. The F-14 fired its AIM-54 Phoenix missile, but did not score a kill as the offending MiGs retreated upon detecting the missile launch. Tensions remained high over the next few years, and these aerial cat-and-mouse games continued until the 2003 invasion of Iraq.

Tomcats of Enduring Freedom

O n September 20, 2001, President George W. Bush addressed the American people from the US Capitol and announced, "Tonight, we are country awakened to danger and called to defend freedom. Our grief has turned to anger and anger to resolution." His remarks were in reference to the terrorist attacks on New York City and Washington DC on September 11. It was a dastardly, premeditated act of terror—the likes of which the United States had never seen. This attack on US soil,

On September 12, 2001, the day after the deadly terrorist attacks on New York City and Washington DC, this F-14 aboard the USS *Enterprise* takes flight for an aerial patrol near the Arabian Sea. Within weeks, the naval air squadrons aboard the *Enterprise* would be fully-engaged in the bombardment of Afghanistan—targeting al-Qaeda and the Taliban regime that harbored its ranks. (US Navy)

In October 2001, a flight deck crewman readies an F-14 for action in what will become the opening stages of the air campaign against al-Qaeda and the Taliban. (US Navy)

perpetrated by the al-Qaeda terrorist group, rallied the country to retaliate. In the weeks following September 11, the recurring themes of "justice" and "freedom" resounded through America's political discourse. These concepts stood in direct contrast to the radical, Islamic fundamentalism of al-Qaeda and the countries that harbored its ranks.

In the case of September 11, al-Qaeda had been aided and abetted by the Taliban regime—a brutal Islamic theocracy that had taken over Afghanistan in the wake of the Soviets' departure. President Bush continued highlighting the contrast between the freedoms of the West and the brutality of the Taliban as he declared the start of a "Global War on Terror."

The United States was now on the offensive.

Likewise, President Bush declared that, going forward, "any nation that continues to harbor or support terrorism will be regarded by the United States as a hostile regime." Approximately two weeks later, the first American airstrikes began in Afghanistan—the official start of Operation Enduring Freedom.

Leading up to these airstrikes, however, the US demanded the immediate closing of training camps in Afghanistan and the deliverance of al-Qaeda leader Osama Bin Laden to US authorities. "These demands are not open to negotiation or discussion," said President Bush. "The Taliban must act and act immediately. They will hand over the terrorists, or they will share in their fate."

All told, the US knew that the Taliban would never comply with these demands. Thus, as early as September 12, the Department of Defense began discussing its options for war. Given Afghanistan's location, responsibility for theater-level operations would fall to the United States Central Command (CENTCOM). CENTCOM determined that a combination of efforts were needed to make headway in Afghanistan—air power, Special Forces, and building alliances with indigenous militant groups opposed to the Taliban. Al-Qaeda and the Taliban were unconventional enemies; thus the US needed an unconventional approach. Unlike during Desert Storm, American forces were not fighting a conventional near-peer threat; this time the enemy was an unconventional group hiding both in the wilderness and amongst the population. As Secretary of Defense Donald Rumsfeld said: "There's no question that there are any number of people in Afghanistan - tribes in the south and the Northern Alliance in the north - that oppose the Taliban, and clearly we need to recognize the value they bring to this anti-terrorist, anti-Taliban effort, and where possible find ways to assist them."

Much of this assistance would come from the skies. And the F-14's newfound bombing capability was put to its most fervent use yet. Due to Afghanistan's landlocked position between Iran and Pakistan (and Pakistan's reluctance to let US forces launch from its territory), the best avenue of approach was from the northern Arabian Sea. Luckily, America had no shortage of tactical aircraft capable of flying that distance—including the B-1 Lancer, B-2 Stealth Bomber, and the F-14 Tomcat.

By October 2001, the USS *Enterprise* and USS *Carl Vinson*, with their F-14s and F/A-18s aboard, stood at the edge of the Arabian Sea, awaiting their orders to strike. Those orders arrived on October 7, when President Bush announced: "The United States military has begun strikes against al-Qaida terrorist camps and military installations of the Taliban regime in Afghanistan. These carefully targeted actions are designed to

Armed with two AIM-9 Sidewinder missiles, a Paveway II Laser-Guided GBU-10 bomb, and a LANTIRN Pod, this F-14D Tomcat prepares for a bombing mission over Afghanistan on November 7, 2001. (US Navy)

disrupt the use of Afghanistan as a terrorist base of operations, and to attack the military capability of the Taliban regime."

The F-14's mission was to strike these "military installations"—including air bases, missile sites, barracks, ammunition depots, and training camps. Although the United States led the operation, the fight against the Taliban quickly became a NATO mission—including contributions from Great Britain, Canada, Germany and France. Alongside these stalwart allies were several non-NATO partners—more than 40 countries that granted airspace usage and landing rights to coalition aircraft.

During the preparations for Enduring Freedom, Lieutenant Commander Bill Lind, a Tomcat RIO, was awestruck by the scope of the operation. He later said that the overall plan for the air campaign was "as large as it was audacious." Indeed, according to Lind:

> "This was to be no pinprick retaliatory strike. This was a campaign centered on air power. Providing me with yet another sense of the unreal, if this plan were to come to fruition, it would see US naval air power let off the leash like no time since World War II. We would have full tanker support over Afghanistan, as well as AWACS coverage from overhead in Pakistan, and the target list eliminated not only the limited command and control nodes of the Taliban and al-Qaida, but just about every piece of military gear and potential military site in the country."

When Operation Enduring Freedom began, there were three F-14 squadrons available, with 33 Tomcats among them. From the outset of the air campaign, B-1s and B-52s struck the Taliban's early warning radar sites and air defense targets. Squadron VF-213, with its sturdy fleet of Tomcats, then opened the airstrikes on military targets with their F-14Ds. Ordnanceman CWO3 Michael Lavoie noted after arming these Tomcats, that

On Christmas Day 2001, as the fighting in Afghanistan intensifies, this F-14 from VF-211 launches from the flight deck of the USS *John C. Stennis*. (US Navy)

An F-14 refuels over Afghanistan in between one of its many bombing runs. Like in Bosnia and during Operation Desert Fox, the F-14 made extensive use of its ground attack capabilities. It highlighted the versatility of the Tomcat, and gave the F-14's advocates another data point upon which to argue that the plane was still useful to America's military. (US Navy)

"we uploaded bombs in quantities that we had never previously hung on a VF-213 aircraft – two of the Tomcats carried pairs of 1000-lb GBU-16s, and the remaining jets were armed with 500-lb GBU-12s. We also armed each of them with single AIM-54C Phoenix and AIM-7M Sparrow missiles, as well as two AIM-9L Sidewinders and 678 rounds for their 20mm cannon." The additional weight was a concern for the crews, as it could affect the Tomcat's range. With this additional weight, even getting off the flight deck was a bit of a concern. The catapults would have to be calibrated accordingly.

During their inaugural missions, the F-14Ds were going to lead two squadrons in a simultaneous three-squadron attack. These Tomcats would be supplemented by two F/A-18Cs, an EA-6B, and two B-1s. The F-14s' first target was in the east: a missile site and support facility near Kabul International Airport. The third squadron was a pure F/A-18 unit, and was to hit the Kandahar airfield. As all three squadrons approached their target, the Hornets were to first launch their Standoff Land Attack Missiles (SLAM-ERs) from fifty nautical miles. Upon detonation, the Taliban knew they were under attack and fired off a surprising amount of Anti-Aircraft Artillery (AAA). Lieutenant Commander Peterson noted, "The Taliban may not have had more than one radar-guided SAM guarding Kabul, but these guys had a sh★tload of AAA! It looked like you could get out of the jet and walk across it." To avoid the anti-aircraft fire, the F-14s climbed higher and lined up their targets again. Once in range, they dropped their GBU-12s on a Taliban missile site and cleared the airspace for the trailing B-1s who were flying in to complete the attack and destroy what was left.

Taxiing prior to its launch, an F-14 from VF-211 "Checkmates," prepares for action on January 8, 2002. (US Navy)

Meanwhile, as these events unfolded in the skies over Kabul, Squadron VF-213 was near Herat in western Afghanistan, escorting the B-1 bombers as they decimated the local air base. After the B-1s delivered their bombs, the F-14s then vectored off to destroy a communications facility with their laser guided bombs (LGB). Delivering "smart weapons" such as these were well within the Tomcat's forte. Commander Anthony Giaini, a seasoned F-14 pilot, explained the Tomcat's purpose even further when he stated:

"The strike I led on the first night of the war reflected both the realities imposed on us by the limited number of assets we could support, the ranges involved and the kind of enemy we faced. Unless, and until, we could eliminate the air defenses in Afghanistan, the tankers would not be going in-country. The result was that the Tomcats hit the far targets in Kabul and Herat and the Hornets hit the nearer ones in and around Kandahar. In reality, all three locations were a real stretch, requiring precise planning, absolute discipline and jets kept in top shape. We were blessed to have all three. In fact, I would go so far as to say that range and endurance were as much a weapon as the LGBs we carried - without the Tomcat's ability to reach distant targets and return to the tankers un-refueled, the campaign might have lasted much longer."

Commander Giaini's point was well taken. The location of the targets inside Afghanistan would have been nearly unreachable for any other fighter. During these opening volleys of the war, the F-14 found itself in the right place at the right time—providing a high-endurance, highly-armed airframe that fit the needs for a deep-strike effort. In fact, in a reversal of fortunes from the early days of Desert Storm, US Navy aircraft flew more

An F-14 Tomcat (left) and F/A-18 Hornet (right), both from Carrier Air Wing 9, prepare to launch from the deck of the USS *John C. Stennis* for another combat mission over Afghanistan—February 2002.

than 70 percent of all strike missions from the start of Enduring Freedom on October 7 until the end of December 2001. All told, it was the most precise naval bombing effort in American history, due largely to the Tomcat's upgraded LANTIRN and laser-guided bomb systems.

In the opening days of the campaign, American F-14s achieved a hit rate of nearly one hundred percent. Over the next several weeks, their mission remained the same: long-range destruction of Taliban barracks, bunker busting, and engaging surface-to-air missile sites. Spanning distances of nearly 700 nautical miles and lasting nearly ten hours in duration, these missions pushed the limits of what was possible for the F-14. Naval air squadrons flew nearly 40 combat missions a day. The F-14s had no issue making the 1,400-mile round trip, but the F/A-18s needed in-flight refueling. As the air war over Afghanistan progressed into its second week, the USS *Enterprise* and *Carl Vinson* were joined by the *Theodore Roosevelt* on October 15, 2001, followed by the USS *John C. Stennis* and USS *Kitty Hawk* several weeks later. All five carriers took turns sending sorties on day-and-night rotations, working approximately 16-hour days.

During these early days of Operation Enduring Freedom, nearly 93 percent of weapons delivered were precision-guided—including the 2,000lb GBU-31 Joint Direct Attack Munition (JDAM); the 1,000-lb GBU-16 Paveway II (LGB); the AGM-65 tactical air-to-ground missile; and the AGM-84 Standoff Land Attack Missile- Extended Range (SLAM-ER). After two weeks of bombing strategic targets—including air defense sites, airfields, mountainside bunkers, and training camps—the campaign shifted its focus onto tactical ground-attack operations and providing close air support to anti-Taliban alliance groups.

Tora Bora

By the end of 2001, the United States had seen a shift in the Taliban's operations. With many of their facilities destroyed, both al-Qaeda and the Taliban fled into the mountainous caves of eastern Afghanistan—to a region known as Tora Bora. The hasty retreat had come as no surprise to the US. In fact, President Bush had anticipated it in his speech of September 20—noting, "the terrorists may burrow deeper into caves and other entrenched hiding places. Our military action is also designed to clear the way for sustained, comprehensive and relentless operations to drive them out and bring them to justice."

The caves of Tora Bora were well-known for their defensive capabilities. In fact, the US had helped the *Mujahedeen* improve Tora Bora's redoubts during the Soviet-Afghan War in the 1980s. Thus, when the Battle of Tora Bora began on December 6, 2001, the Taliban remained confident that their mountainous defenses could withstand any attack from US ground forces. However, al-Qaeda and the Taliban had failed to consider the improved capabilities of the F-14 and her ground-attack stablemates.

For the F-14, the Tora Bora missions took on a slightly different nature than the ones completed in months prior. In fact, according to the chief maintenance officer of Squadron VF-102:

> "The Tora Bora sorties proved challenging for us, as we were essentially trying to hit little more than a rock blocking a cave entrance in very rugged terrain at high altitude right on the Afghan-Pakistan border. The close proximity of the latter meant that we could not spill out into Pakistani airspace after making bombing runs. Breaking out the key rock that needed to be bombed through the FLIR (forward-looking infrared) when it was the same color as its surrounding proved a virtually impossible task. Things became even worse at night, as at least during the day you could talk to your RIO and the ground controller about what they were seeing. The location of the troops on the ground was not ideal either, as they tended to be further away from the cave entrances that needed bombing than we would have liked - this was particularly the case at night. Occasionally, you would see enemy troops moving in the Tora Bora area, and the LTS also picked up the hotspots of activity."

These missions, however, were critical to assisting US-led ground forces, clearing paths and dropping LGBs on enemy-held terrain. Typically, Tomcats engaged these ground targets with the GBU-12 and laser-guided systems. As a general rule, the US was hesitant to use anything other than precision-guided munitions due to the risk of fratricide. Thus, the F-14, with its onboard optics and state-of-the-art weaponry became a regular sight in the skies over Afghanistan. Many times, however, the F-14s still needed assistance when engaging targets. One such occasion occurred on December 12, 2001, when VF-102 was called upon to suppress a large number of al-Qaida and Taliban fighters within the Tora Bora cave complexes. As one pilot described it:

> "As was often the case in the night missions during the Tora Bora campaign, we had an AC-130 gunship mark the cave entrances for us. My female RIO and I could not break out the targets that we were supposed to be bombing even with the LTS, so the "Spooky" [common nickname for the AC-130] crew used their humongous

On February 26, 2003, as the Iraq War looms on the horizon, an F-14D from Squadron VF-213 launches from the flight deck of the USS *Theodore Roosevelt*, conducting another mission in support of Operation Enduring Freedom. (US Navy)

suite of targeting sensors at a considerably lower altitude than us to pick out the cave entrances amongst the rocks in the area. When we asked them to mark the target for us, they fired "Willie Pete" [White Phosphorus] unguided rockets directly at the cave entrances that needed to be bombed. They were flying with all their lights off, which meant that we could not see them, so I had to wait for the pilot to tell us that they were five miles from the target before we went in and dropped our LGB. The bomb hit the cave and exploded…moments later the hill literally erupted like an ant's nest, as people started scurrying away in all directions– we could clearly see them through the FLIR."

These missions continued until December 17, 2001. Although the objective during the Tora Bora campaign was to capture Osama bin Laden and kill al-Qaeda's senior leadership, US forces did not accomplish either. It was later determined that bin Laden was, in fact, at Tora Bora, but escaped. Although bin Laden remained at large, the fight for Tora Bora had flushed the Taliban from their last defensive position. Following Tora Bora, the F-14s and their carrier flight crews saw little action until the start of Operation Anaconda in March 2002.

Operation Anaconda

Still on the hunt for al-Qaeda leaders and Osama bin Laden, US intelligence looked for

An F-14 assigned to VF-11 makes ready to launch from the flight deck of the USS *John F. Kennedy* in support of ground forces in Afghanistan, March 2002. (US Navy)

regions that would provide attack and defensive positions. In February 2002, analysts began focusing on the lower Shah-i-Kot Valley. Standing at an average elevation of 9,000 feet, this rugged valley had been the site of an intense battle between Soviet Airborne Troops and the *Mujahedeen* in January 1988. Fortified with bunkers and offering excellent redoubts, US analysts believed that enemy forces from Tora Bora had escaped to the Lower Shah-i-Kot Valley and were planning to regroup against the US-led coalition. Thus, American forces began devising a plan to flush the enemy out of the Shah-i-Kot. It was to be called Operation Anaconda.

Anaconda featured a mix of conventional ground forces with close air support. On the ground were 2,000 soldiers from the US Army's 10th Mountain Division and 101st Airborne Division. Additionally, allied Afghan forces supplemented the operation with their own indigenous fighters. This US-Afghan force intended the destruction of all enemy units within seventy-two hours. Operation Anaconda commenced on March 1, 2002, beginning with US Special Forces teams sweeping the outskirts of the valley. Unfortunately for the F-14s, their inclusion in Operation Anaconda was not as well-planned as it had been during the previous campaigns. Due to poor weather, aerial operations started later and, when the F-14 crews were informed of changes, they discovered the airspace coordination was unclear. After the first two days of Anaconda, Lieutenant Commander Nick Dienna noted:

"There had been little coordination between the 10th Mountain Division, which was running the offensive on the ground, and TACAIR assets in-theatre, which were in essence charged with supplying the aerial artillery for the troops. I experienced the lack of big picture airspace and tactical control during the early phase of the offensive at first hand when my section made ten runs through the Shah-i-kot Valley trying to release our weapons. Each time the Apaches came through beneath us working the valley, thus preventing us from getting our ordnance off."

Over the next few days, Army and Navy aircrews de-conflicted the airspace issue. However, American ground forces soon discovered that their intelligence on the valley was wrong. The number of Taliban forces, estimated at approximately 200, was now thought to be 500-1,000. To make matters worse, the Taliban were holding their fortified locations with greater competency than expected. As a result, US-Afghan forces were taking heavier losses than anticipated. Some of the lingering difficulty was caused by the terrain; and some of it was caused by the Taliban's ambushing tactics. Luckily, during these happenstances, the F-14 Tomcat provided some much-needed support.

On March 4, 2002, Squadron VF-211 was on duty when a Navy SEAL team came under fire in the Takur Ghar region, trying to establish observation posts at either end of the Shah-i-kot Valley. Upon arrival, the Taliban fired on the SEAL team's MH-47 Chinook helicopter. As the helicopter attempted to evade enemy fire, it sustained an RPG hit, causing SEAL Petty Officer Neil C. Roberts to fall out of the helicopter's now-opened ramp. Army Rangers, aboard two other Chinooks, responded to extract Roberts

Another day, another sortie. Such was the routine for the air crews of Squadron VF-2 "Bounty Hunters" during their 2002 deployment in support of both Operation Enduring Freedom and Southern Watch. Within the year, however, Southern Watch would give way to Operation Iraqi Freedom, the US-led invasion to topple the regime of Saddam Hussein. (US Navy)

At the twilight of its service, the F-14 Tomcat continued to serve in the skies over Afghanistan until November 2003. With the Tomcat's retirement now less than three years away, the Navy withdrew its Tomcats from Enduring Freedom and sent its remaining F-14s into the skies over Iraq. These air support missions over Iraq would be the Tomcat's last hurrah in US naval service. (US Navy)

but, upon their arrival, one of their helicopters was shot down, killing four crewmen. The survivors of the event hunkered down in defensive positions, approximately 150 meters from an al-Qaida bunker. To assist the beleaguered operators, a call went out to four F-14s from VF-211, flying near Takur Ghar.

Pilot Lieutenant Dan Buchar recalled the event:

"Shortly after dawn, I launched as part of a division of four F-14s sent into Afghanistan in support of Anaconda, having been briefed to head to the Shah-i-kot Valley to help troops in contact as they continued to battle with enemy forces. As we headed north, the SOF MH-47E was shot down near Objective Ginger. Shortly after that, our division lead, Lt. Larry Sidbury, got a call from 'Bossman' telling him that our bombs were needed straight away. We had to refuel first, however, so each jet quickly topped off its tanks and then headed independently to the target area. Lt. Sidbury and RIO, Lt Commander Tim Fitzpatrick, who were both FAC(A) qualified, reached Takur Ghar first and made contact with 'Slick 01.' The latter was pinned down near the wreckage of the MH-47 along with the survivors of the Army Ranger quick reaction unit. Lt. Sidbury and his wingman, Lt. Bryan Roberts, worked directly with 'Slick 01,' and they dropped ordnance within 500 meters of the friendlies."

Due, in part, to the aerial cover provided by the Tomcats above, these Special Operations troops escaped the melee and were ultimately rescued. Although Operation Anaconda was a tactical victory for American forces, it highlighted the need for tight inter-service communication and better intelligence. An operation intended to last 72 hours ended up running a total of eighteen days. The US saw eight servicemen killed, 72 wounded, and lost two Chinook helicopters. In the end, US forces pushed the Taliban and al-Qaida from the valley, but Osama bin Laden remained at large and no major captures or kills had been confirmed.

The Tomcat's End of Mission

By 2003, with the Taliban having been degraded to a "minimal threat," the Navy began sending most of its Tomcat squadrons home. The Tomcat's effect had clearly been felt; and the F-14's impact on the mission's success could not be denied. However, with the impending retirement of the F-14 quickly approaching, its role in Operation Enduring Freedom seemed to be somewhat of a swan song.

Nevertheless, these latter-day Tomcats squadrons were proud of their success.

The mission in Afghanistan showed that the F-14 had successfully transitioned from an air superiority fighter to a deadly precision bomber. Squadron VF-211 alone had dropped nearly 100,000 pounds of ordnance throughout Enduring Freedom—much of it during Operation Anaconda. The squadron flew 1,250 missions, logged 4,200 hours in combat, and had a sortie completion rate of 99.7 percent.

As most F-14 squadrons departed Afghanistan, VF-11 and VF-211 stayed behind as the final squadrons. Ground forces remained active, but the fixed-wing air support became a lower priority for the Navy. Indeed, as time went on, the Air Force's A-10 Warthogs, F-15E Strike Eagles, and AC-130 gunships assumed most of the responsibility in that realm. Over time, the F-14s were relegated to random tanker strikes and fly-bys to show a presence in the area. The fly-by, however, was something new for the Tomcat. As Commander John Aquilino noted :

"This was not a mission that we had been trained to fly pre-cruise, as it had never appeared in our work-up syllabus. We had been told by VF-102 during our OEF turnover that fly-bys would soon feature regularly in our mission tasking. VF-211 emphasized this point too, explaining to us that although such fly-bys may not have seemed to be too big a deal from the crew's perspective, they meant a lot to the soldiers on the ground. When crowds were gathering near troops in patrol, and their intention was unknown, the fact that there were US jets in the air overhead that could have a direct impact on the situation was greatly appreciated by Coalition forces.

With months of experience in-country, our troops had supplied the CAOC [Combined Air Operations Center] with feedback via 'Bossman' on how they could get the most value out of our fly-bys. We were told that it was crucial to find an area near to the disturbance where the jet's engines could clearly be heard—it didn't matter if the aircraft could not actually be seen by friendly troops. A successful fly-by was one that dispersed a crowd or helped buy the soldiers time to get a better understanding of what the crowd was going to do. I was asked to perform just one show-of-force fly-by, and this was during a marathon ten-hour daylight mission. Patrolling northern Afghanistan, we were assigned a CAP station and a frequency for a ground FAC. Having checked in with him, we then waited during our window to provide this guy with whatever he needed—weapons on target, a show-of-force or just a presence in the sky above him.

After 20 minutes of silence, he got back on the radio and asked us to fly a show-of-force. He passed us the latitude and longitude for the fly-by, what direction he wanted us to come in from, the height we were cleared down to and any known threats in the area. We set up our jets in a two airplane defensive spread for mutual support and optimum threat coverage, and then each of us took it in turns to make a single high-speed, subsonic pass with the afterburners 'cooking' so as to make lots of noise."

These fly-by missions continued over the next several months, with a few more combat missions involving strikes against ground targets. However, in November 2003, VF-211 became the final F-14 squadron to fly a mission over Afghanistan. As part of Operation Mountain Resolve, Lieutenant Dan Buchar recalled:

"The CAOC wanted one FAC(A) crew per section over the beach, and that really hit a small number of our naval aviators hard. VF-211 only had four suitably qualified crews at the time. I pulled the 0200 hrs to 0800 hrs FAC(A) watch with my RIO, which was not a lot of fun. CVW-1 [Carrier Air Wing 1] ran the FAC window at night and Bagram-based A-10s ran it during the day. I got to fly a couple of show-of-force passes during this period, where we were cleared down to 3,000 ft— these were the standout missions for me during the twelve days that we supported Mountain Resolve. We flew some very long sorties lasting more than hours at a time, and I undertook three of these in a 72-hour period, all at night, as the CAOC wanted round-the-clock FAC(A) cover in theatre. They set up E-2C and EA-6B dets [detachments] at Bagram in support of Mountain Resolve, but had the TACAIR assets flying from the boat. The operation was well executed by CVW-1, but our troops failed to find any worthwhile targets for us to bomb."

So ended the Tomcat's role in Operation Enduring Freedom. The F-14 flew its last patrol in Afghanistan on November 14, 2003. Although the F-14 had already been scheduled for retirement in 2006, the Tomcat's mission in the Middle East was far from over. Even as it continued patrolling the skies of Afghanistan, the Tomcat would soon join the effort known as Operation Iraqi Freedom.

Tomcats of Iraqi Freedom

Continuing the Global War on Terror, the United States then turned its attention towards Iraq. Under the newly-articulated Bush Doctrine, the United States would pursue a policy of pre-emptive action against any country that harbored terrorists or likely posed a threat to American security. "If we wait for threats to fully materialize," the President said, "we will have waited too long." To this end, the US prosecuted its case against Saddam Hussein's Iraq.

Following the end of the Gulf War in 1991, US-Iraqi relations remained at an all-time low. The economic sanctions and No-Fly Zones were only the most visible reminders

An F-14 ignites its afterburners, preparing to launch from the flight deck aboard the USS *Kitty Hawk*. Embarked as a member of Carrier Air Wing Five, this F-14 is one of several conducting aerial combat missions in support of Operation Iraqi Freedom, March 2003. (US Navy)

In support of the "Shock and Awe" aerial campaign against Saddam Hussein, this F-14 Tomcat from Squadron VF-213 "Black Lions" launches from the USS *Theodore Roosevelt* on the night of March 21, 2003. (US Navy)

of this lingering animosity. Indeed, since his defeat at the hands of the US military, Saddam had increased his support for terrorism, and orchestrated a number of terror plots himself. One audacious plot involved an assassination attempt on former President George HW Bush. To make matters worse, Saddam had defied multiple UN sanctions and expelled UN weapons inspectors from Iraq. Thus, it came as little surprise when the international community renewed its interest in assessing Iraq's ability to create Weapons of Mass Destruction (WMD). These weapons included Mustard Gas, VX, Sarin, and the normal variety of nuclear munitions.

To initiate action against Iraq, however, the United States had to build the case for an invasion. Working with the United Nations, a series of weapons factory inspections took place in Iraq throughout 2002. In turn, the UN passed resolutions demanding Iraq's disarmament. The weapons inspection, however, yielded inconclusive results. The inspectors recorded several abnormalities and oddly-missing components that were vital to the creation of WMDs. Meanwhile, Deputy Secretary of Defense Paul Wolfowitz conceded that there were other concerns:

"The truth is that, for reasons that have a lot to do with the US government bureaucracy, we settled on the one issue that everyone could agree on, which was weapons of mass destruction as the core reason, but, there have always been three fundamental concerns. One is weapons of mass destruction, the second is support for terrorism, the third is the criminal treatment of the Iraqi people. Actually I guess you could say there's a fourth overriding one which is the connection between the first two."

With his purpose clear, President Bush looked to Congress for approval. Before a joint session of Congress, Bush argued that "the gathering threat of Iraq must be confronted fully and finally." Thus, on October 3, 2002, the House and Senate authorized the use of military force against Iraq.

Having received Congressional approval, Bush then sent Secretary of State Colin Powell to the United Nations, accelerating America's effort to gain the blessing of the international community. On February 5, 2003, in front of the UN General Assembly, Powell artfully presented his case. He argued that, "the moment we find ourselves in now is a critical moment where we are being tested and where the Security Council of the United Nations and the international community is being tested." He provided what seemed like evidence that Iraq was still manufacturing WMDs. Powell further argued that Saddam's defiance of past resolutions would undermine the UN's credibility. Accordingly, he warned that the United Nations would become "irrelevant if it passes resolution after resolution that is simply totally ignored by a country in a situation where that country continues to develop weapons of mass destruction."

Although sincere and passionate in his presentation, Colin Powell failed to win support from the United Nations. Although there was much dissent within the General Assembly, the US had still won a number of allies to its cause. There would be no UN resolution, but allies such as the United Kingdom and Australia pledged their support. Seemingly undeterred by the UN's lack of enthusiasm, President Bush stated that if Saddam Hussein

On March 22, 2003, from the confines of the Mediterranean Sea, this F-14B launches from one of the four steam-driven catapults aboard the USS *Harry S. Truman*. This Tomcat is departing upon another mission against the now beleaguered forces of Saddam Hussein. (US Navy)

April 2003 – as the bombing campaign goes into its second month, an aging F-14A Tomcat is pulled into position by a tow tractor on the flight deck of the USS *Kitty Hawk*. Minutes away from launching, this F-14 is scheduled to perform another mission in support of Operation Iraqi Freedom. (US Navy)

did not disarm, the United States would "lead a coalition of the willing to disarm him and at that point in time, all our nations…will be able to choose whether or not they want to participate." This "coalition of the willing" eventually grew to include more than 40 allies. Meanwhile, CIA operatives and Special Forces troops had been in Iraq for months, performing reconnaissance and preparing for what would become Operation Iraqi Freedom.

The military invasion of Iraq began on March 20, 2003 and had a wide-sweeping agenda with eight objectives. According to US Army General Tommy Franks, these objectives were as follows:

"First, ending the regime of Saddam Hussein. Second, to identify, isolate, and eliminate Iraq's weapons of mass destruction. Third, to search for, to capture, and to drive out terrorists from that country. Fourth, to collect such intelligence as we can relate to terrorist networks. Fifth, to collect such intelligence as we can relate to the global network of illicit weapons of mass destruction. Sixth, to end sanctions and to immediately deliver humanitarian support. Seventh, to secure Iraq's oil fields and resources, which belong to the Iraqi people. And last, to help the Iraqi people create conditions for a transition to a representative self-government."

While simple in theory, these objectives would embroil the US into a divisive seven-year conflict.

For the F-14 Tomcat, however, Operation Iraqi Freedom presented another opportunity to engage a conventional enemy. With its scope of duties expanded from

An F-14 receives its combat load for another strike operation in Iraq – March 30, 2003. (US Navy)

patrol and recon, to active engagement and bombing runs, the emerging "Second Gulf War" highlighted the ongoing utility of the F-14. The recent upgrades to Joint Direct Attack Munitions (JDAMs) and Laser-Guided Bombs (LGBs) would prove vital to the F-14s. The JDAM was particularly vital, as it was now the weapon of choice. Since the JDAM was fully autonomous upon deployment, its accuracy percentages were even greater than the LGBs. For the Tomcat's aircrews, however, Operation Iraqi Freedom was a bittersweet mission—it would be the last operational deployment of the F-14 before its retirement in 2006.

The beginning of Operation Iraqi Freedom was termed "Shock and Awe"—a series of precision airstrikes targeting key Iraqi command and control nodes. According to Navy Captain Mark Fox:

"The plan called for an air campaign kicked off with a massive air strike ('A-Day,' and the beginning of 'Shock and Awe'), followed a few days later by the ground war ('G-Day'). The plan evolved, however, as the conflict grew nearer. The gap between 'A-' and 'G-Days' grew progressively smaller, with good reason - days of heavy air strikes would give the Iraqis the opportunity to sabotage their domestic oilfields and offshore oil platforms before our ground forces could intervene. The opening strike - consisting of multiple salvos of cruise missiles and Coalition strike aircraft - targeted hundreds of aim points in several sequential waves, making the first hours of OIF the most overwhelming delivery of precision ordnance ever seen. Designed to saturate and destroy Iraqi air defenses, roll back the Baghdad Super Missile Exclusion Zone (SuperMEZ), destroy key command and control nodes and degrade the ground

Two F-14D Tomcats armed with 500-pound GBU-12 bombs, fly in formation on a combat sortie over Iraq – April 21, 2004. (US Navy)

forces' ability to defend Baghdad, the opening strike was pretty impressive for a single evening's work."

Meanwhile, in the United States, President Bush announced the commencement of Operation Iraqi Freedom. In a televised address from the Oval Office, Bush delivered his message to the American people:

"On my orders, coalition forces have begun striking selected targets of military importance to undermine Saddam Hussein's ability to wage war...These are the opening stages of what will be a broad and concerted campaign. Our nation enters this conflict reluctantly, yet our purpose is sure. The people of the United States and our friends and allies will not live at the mercy of an outlaw regime that threatens the peace with weapons of mass murder. We will meet that threat now with our army, air force, navy, coast guard and marines so that we do not have to meet it later with armies of firefighters and police and doctors on the streets of our cities. Now that conflict has come, the only way to limit its duration is to apply decisive force and I assure you this will not be a campaign of half measures and we will accept no outcome but victory."

Thus, the Iraq War began.

Navy Captain Doug Denneny, a distinguished Tomcat RIO and the Executive Officer of Squadron VF-2 recalled his first few days in the air campaign of Operation Iraqi Freedom:

"I was fortunate enough to participate in the first mission of OIF as a division lead, controlling two Tomcats and two Hornets. My CO was designated as the overall strike lead for an operation scheduled to take place later that day, so as per standard procedure in a frontline squadron, the CO and the XO were assigned separate missions. We had been tasked with dropping JDAM on the Ministry of Information's Salman Pak radio relay transmitter facility at Al Hurriyah, southwest of central Baghdad, and in order to effectively employ our ordnance we had to fly into the infamous Super MEZ which ringed the city. This had become legendary amongst naval aviators during the years of OSW [Operation Southern Watch], as the overlapping rings of IADS [Integrated Air Defense Systems] around Baghdad were so dense that they effectively blotted out the city itself whenever color printouts of the Iraqi capital were produced for threat analysis purposes!"

As the F-14s approached Salman Pak, they witnessed Baghdad being pummeled by a variety of Coalition ordnance. Indeed, the F/A-18s and F-16CJs were delivering their own bombs, preventing Iraqi air defenses from firing on the F-14s. These suppression efforts worked at first, but the enemy's air defense batteries were soon returning fire. Faced with the decision to abort the mission or press on with the attack, Captain Denneny chose the latter. His pilot on this mission was Lieutenant Commander Kurt Frankenberger, who remembered the operation as such:

"As we pressed towards the target in what would be a clockwise flow north, then east, then south, we could see the initial TLAM, CALCM and Stealth aircraft weapons impacting in the distance. Our wingman took some great video footage, documenting the target ingress as if he was going to Disneyland - this later made

Following a long day of combat missions, the sun sets behind an F-14 Tomcat from VF-32, "The Fighting Swordsmen." (US Navy)

for a nice CNN tape. A medium altitude cloud layer occasionally obscured the lights of Baghdad, but with or without NVGs, the city could be seen getting hit regularly. This was my first combat experience in 17 years of service with the Navy, and my level of anxiety was high.

As the flight lead of a mixed division of two F-14Ds and two F/A-18Cs, we solved some timing issues and flowed from our Initial Point (IP) on into the target for weapons release. During the 25-mile run from the IP west of Baghdad to the release point, we observed so many SAM launches (10+) that we couldn't count them anymore. Effectively, we had to trust our systems and visually confirm that each missile did not appear to be tracking, then disregard it and evaluate the next one. The more alarming sights were the HARM rounds that were launched from the four F-16CJs behind us. These came out of nowhere and into sight very close to our altitude. You needed to recall the location of the shooter and listen up for the launching calls.

JDAM delivery went as advertised from our aircraft, although our wingman's jet had a weapons system failure which powered down the JDAM just as he attempted to release his bombs. We kept the speed up for egress and continued to monitor the threat, with constant SAM launches and AAA going off below us to light up the night sky. The explosions from our weapons were also evident, although the cloud partially obscured them. Then the normal admin issues came back into play—worrying about gas and weather at the tanker, making your recovery slot over the shop and, of course, the gratuitous night trap."

Prepped by its deck handlers, this F-14B from VF-32 prepares for another combat mission from aboard the USS *Harry S Truman*. (US Navy)

A pair of F-14 Tomcat from Squadron VF-143 "Pukin' Dogs" fly over Iraq on July 3, 2004. This was VF-143's last deployment with the F-14 Tomcat. Upon returning home later that month, VF-143 transitioned to the F/A-18 Hornet and was re-designated VFA-143, indicating its new role as a fighter-attack squadron. (US Navy)

In the days that followed, the ground invasion of Iraq launched from neighboring Kuwait. Despite heavy resistance, coalition troops reached Baghdad within two weeks.

Meanwhile, in the skies, American Tomcats continued propagating the "Shock and Awe" campaign. In total, twenty F-14s from Squadron VF-2 and VF-31 participated, delivering their JDAMs and GBU-31s, both to great effect. In fact, according to Lieutenant Commander Dave Grogan, the JDAM was so effective that it may have been too easy. "JDAM was such a simple system to use," he said, "that you could almost have put a monkey in the front seat of a Tomcat and it would have flown a satisfactory mission profile to ensure the weapon's accurate delivery!" Grogan even remarked that the weapon's delivery was almost anti-climactic given the paltry air defense operations mounted by the Iraqis. Grogan continued:

"The most important aspect of a JDAM mission for the crew was making sure that we had the target coordinates correctly copied down - these were given to us either in the pre-launch brief or once we were over Iraq. Both the RIO and I would double-check the coordinates before they were dialed into the bomb via the mission computer. From my OSW/OIF experience, I would suggest that the only weak point in the whole JDAM system is the data entry phase. The actual drop zone for the JDAM from its maximum range was usually quite large, so we would take it to the heart of the target area whenever possible before hitting the release switch. In the Tomcat community, we were so used to having to visually identify the target with the LTS and the FLIR before hitting the 'pickle button' to release an LGB that

An F-14 on another combat mission over Iraq, August 2004. (US Air Force)

it initially felt rather odd to be expending JDAM through solid cloud against targets that we never saw."

To support the ground attack, the F-14 and its support crews switched to a "kill box" system. This would allow the ground commanders to designate a specific area "closed" or "open" to air strikes depending on the proximity of friendly ground troops. With these designations, the F-14 air strikes were moving into the Forward Air Controller (Airborne), or FAC(A), configuration—much as they had done during Operation Allied Force in Kosovo. To this end, the F-14Ds from Squadron VF-2 were particularly useful. One such VF-2 crewman was Lieutenant Commander Mike Peterson, who described a FAC(A) mission on April 10, 2003:

"I launched off of *Constellation*, which we affectionately called 'Satan's Flagship'— being one of the last conventional carriers, it always had a head of 'Brimstone' streaming out of the top stacks. Due to our wingman suffering mechanical problems, and higher priority missions being filled by the spare Tomcat, we proceeded on our mission as a FAC(A) as a single aircraft. Working as a FAC(A), you usually had mutual support from the other CAS [Close Air Support] aircraft operating in any particular area, and having two sets of eyes in the cockpit helped our lookout for surface fires.

After refueling, we were assigned to a kill box by the DASC in support of a 1st MEF [Marine Expeditionary Force] convoy that was working just east of the Tigris River in downtown Baghdad. As we headed on station, I pulled out a 1:50,000 chart and noted the coordinates where we were tasked to be working. It was a location in a dense urban area, just east of a bridge crossing the Tigris. I marked the location on the chart and used the Tomcat's 'moving map feature' to show it to the pilot—in other words, I handed the map with my writing on it up the right side of the cockpit to my pilot!

When we arrived on station, we were contacted by a section of A-10 Warthogs that had just checked in as CAS assets. The convoy had stopped about a block east of the bridge and had surrounded what appeared to be a mosque. There were the typical spires and significant wall surrounding the complex, which was located on the southwest side of an intersection. Apparently, the Marines were planning on looking for high-level Iraqi regime members that may have been hiding in the buildings. Immediately prior to our arrival overhead, the column had been fired on by heavy weapons and rocket-propelled grenades from the group of buildings located to the east side of the complex, across the street at their rear flank. They had sustained some casualties, and were trying to talk the A-10 onto the location of the heaviest fire as the troops pulled back toward the bridge.

We quickly checked in as a FAC(A) and put the LTS to work scouring the mosque complex. We saw the buildings where the enemy fire was coming from after listening to the talk-on by the ground FAC. We were unable to drop our LGBs onto the buildings, however, as the Marines were still nearby, conducting their withdrawal from the area. The A-10 pilot was having a difficult time picking out the correct area to strafe, so we coordinated with the ground FAC and jumped in with a quick talk-on from the aerial perspective, dictating that he make a north-south run on the buildings—parallel to a line of Marine Humvees—with his cannon.

Once we verified that the Air Force pilot had the correct area in his sights, we crossed behind him as he was lining up for his attack run to make certain that he was pointed at the correct group of buildings, before handing final clearance control back to the Marines on the ground. With the friendly troops so close to the buildings, it was better that they had the final say that he wasn't pointed at them if at all possible. The A-10 pilot walked a line of 30mm rounds right down the top of the buildings from which the Marines were receiving the majority of the fire. That enabled them to effectively break contact and move back toward the bridge, and away from the mosque complex. Both A-10s then headed off-station as they had hit bingo fuel state.

An M1A2 Abrams main battle tank then moved up and sat across from the complex in the position where the Marine convoy had initially been located. After a few minutes, additional fire was directed at the M1A2 from a building opposite the mosque. The tank crew replied in kind, firing a single round into the building in an effort to silence the fires in that area, before moving back towards the bridge.

At this point the ground FAC relayed to us that he and his troops were no longer taking fire, and that he was going to call in some artillery while they regrouped, before attempting to enter the mosque complex once again. We decided to make a quick run to the tanker at this point, topping off for maximum on-station time. By the time we had re-established ourselves on-station over central Baghdad, the convoy had regrouped after the initial attack, pushed down the road past the mosque complex and was now flanked by a series of buildings to their right on the south side of the road. The Marines had received additional fire from the buildings and had now stopped a safe distance away. Not wanting to trade fire with a well-entrenched enemy, the Marines instructed us to take out the buildings from which they had been shot at.

We followed the talk-on by the ground FAC and made a dry run to confirm his position, and the exact building that he wanted attacked. The Marines were right on the edge of the acceptable distance for us to put down a 500-lb LGB, so we told them to prepare for the pass, and get everyone's heads down. We delivered a delayed-fused LGB into the last building on the block as instructed and then set up to the west for another attack. The ground control indicated a direct hit, and instructed us to walk our next LGBs one building toward the west, closer to their position. We made two more runs, delivering one bomb each time and walking them down the line of the buildings where the convoy had received fire."

Less than two months after the start of Operation Iraqi Freedom, on May 1, 2003, President George W. Bush donned a flight suit and buckled himself into the passenger seat of an S-3 Viking jet. Landing on the flight deck of the USS *Abraham Lincoln*, Bush became the first sitting president to make an arrested landing on a carrier deck. Emerging from the S-3, Bush delivered a speech to the crew of the *Abraham Lincoln* (and to the millions of Americans watching at home) announcing the success of American forces in Iraq, with a large banner in the background stating "Mission Accomplished."

The President began his speech: "In the battle of Iraq, the United States and our allies have prevailed. And now our coalition is engaged in securing and reconstructing that country." Bush was quick to caveat, however, that: "We have difficult work to do in Iraq.

An F-14B Tomcat, assigned to VF-32, prepares to land on the flight deck aboard the USS Harry S. Truman, following another reconnaissance mission over Iraq. Throughout its service in the Iraq War, F-14s provided close air support, surveillance, and reconnaissance over Iraq. (US Navy)

Banking away from its aerial refueler, this F-14B Tomcat from Squadron VF-103 vectors to continue its mission over Iraq, October 2004. (US Air Force)

We're bringing order to parts of that country that remain dangerous."

Little did anyone know that a brutal insurgency was on the rise.

The ensuing Iraq War would come to define Bush's presidency, while the "Mission Accomplished" banner was later noted for its prematurity and tragic irony.

The insurgency began slowly at first, but quickly gained steam in the area known as the "Sunni Triangle," a highly-populated area with points in Baghdad, Ramadi, and Tikrit. The insurgency came to represent a mix of anti-American, anti-coalition forces—including militias, religious radicals, and Saddam loyalists. Using guerilla tactics—notably IEDs—these insurgents caused considerable trouble for the occupation force. In the wake of this insurgency, however, the US military decided to renew its air strikes as part of a counterinsurgency.

Thus, in 2004, the USS *George Washington* arrived in the Persian Gulf. Aboard its flight bays were two F-14B squadrons: VF-11 and VF-143. It was to be the squadrons' final deployment before their conversion to the F/A-18 Super Hornet. Over the next few months, both squadrons would fly a mix of sorties—including ground attack mission and traditional "show of force" presence patrols.

As the war continued, new carriers arrived in theater. One such carrier was the USS *John F. Kennedy*, with Squadron VF-103 in tow. Flying mixed sorties alongside their F/A-18 brethren, the Tomcats of VF-103 saw plenty of action along the urban battlefronts. Many times, their sorties began as a show of force, but quickly escalated into ground

At the twilight of its career, this F-14 refuels over Iraq from an Air Force KC-10 Extender aircraft from the 908th Expeditionary Refueling Squadron. Within one month, the F-14 Tomcat would see its final combat mission over Iraq. (US Air Force)

attack missions. One such occurrence was described by VF-103 RIO Matt Koop:

"When [Operation] Phantom Fury kicked off, CENTCOM [US Central Command] was concerned that large numbers of foreign fighters would come streaming over the borders from Syria and Iran to aid the insurgency in Fallujah. Coalition forces had set up outposts along these borders to prevent this from happening, and an increase in the number of skirmishes in nearby towns was anticipated. Therefore, sections of fighters were pre-positioned to provide close air support to our troops in these areas if needed. And it was on one of these missions that I saw my first real action of the deployment.

Ironically, when my pilot and I were told that we would be conducting a Syrian border patrol, we were more than a little disappointed not to be working with the Marines in Fallujah, since that was where all the action seemed to be taking place. Our Tomcat was the lead aircraft that afternoon, flying in a mixed section with a Hornet wingman from VFA-81. I checked in with the DASC controller to tell him what our mission was, and where we had been told to patrol—we were hoping that he would give us a last-minute tasking to Fallujah, but that was not to be the case. We continued westward and contacted the JTAC [Joint Tactical Air Controller] that we had been assigned to work with. He described the area that we would be patrolling, and pointed out a few outposts that had intermittently received fire in the previous 48 hours.

Once we were on-station, the troops on the ground duly requested a show of force over their positions to either ward off or stir up any insurgent activity that

While I was working the FLIR in our LTS, my pilot was scouring the streets with and he duty gave us targeting information relating to where the van had last been seen. van. We were told to contact a different JTAC who was actually in the town, and support, and both our section and the helicopters were tasked with locating the blue the insurgents had sped away in their vehicle. The Marines called for immediate air a nearby town had been attacked by terrorists in a blue van. Having exchanged shots, Literally minutes later the JTAC received a report that some of our troops patrolling else popped up.

didn't have any other assignments, so we told him we'd stick around in case anything He told us that if we had any alternate missions, we were cleared to proceed. We "Sorry boys. It just doesn't look like we have much for you fixed-wing guys to do." fast and too high to offer much assistance. It was at this time that the JTAC told us, see a Cobra and a Huey conducting their search below us, but we were flying too and a pair of Marine helicopters had been launched to find the culprits. We could some action. Apparently, two mortar rounds had been launched from a nearby field, When we checked back in, we were disappointed to hear that we had just missed was time to go hit the tanker and top off the tanks.

up and waited for their next request. Everything was still quiet, and after a while it their outposts low, fast and loud. Once we had completed our pass, we climbed back might be brewing nearby. We bumped up the speed and dropped down to overfly

Enterprise. (US Navy)
21, 2004. This is the last time a squadron of F-14s will conduct operations from the flight deck aboard the
An F-14 Tomcat from VF-101 "Grim Reapers" makes its final landing aboard the USS Enterprise on May

his binoculars. We soon spotted the abandoned blue van, and the helicopters came in to confirm that this was indeed the insurgents' vehicle. With this confirmation, the Cobra was cleared to destroy the van with rockets.

While the AH-1W [Cobra helicopter] was firing at the van, new reports were coming in and being passed to us on the radio that additional Marines had been engaged by insurgents who were holed up in a café. The troops had been subjected to both machine gun fire and RPG rounds, and they were in need of immediate air support. This café was less than a kilometer from where we had found the van, and after a quick talk-on by the JTAC, we confirmed that we were 'tally the target.' He then requested that we provide laser designation for a Hellfire missile that was to be fired by the gunner in the Cobra, since his line-of-site for missile guidance was poor. Neither my pilot or I had ever done anything like this before, having never been briefed on how to lase for a Hellfire missile! But we had briefed on buddy lasing for our Hornet wingman's Laser Maverick, and we figured that the two laser-guided weapons were similar enough to expect success if we employed the same tactics. We were right. The Hellfire guided to the dead center of our crosshairs and blew right through the front door of the building. That hit stopped the fire that our troops were receiving, but the weapon's small warhead caused minimal damage to the structure of the building itself.

With the possibility of more insurgents hiding deeper in the café, the order was given for us to destroy the building with our two GBU-12s. We were told to target each end of the building with one bomb, so we would have to make two passes with as little time in between as possible.

As soon as we had received permission to drop our LGBs, we raced out to an appropriate run-in position which minimized the danger posed to our troops nearby. Fortunately, our LTS pod was producing a crisp image, and the target was easily identifiable from more than five miles away. We stepped through the checklist we had memorized and made sure that all our parameters were correct before dropping the first bomb. The weapon guided with perfect precision to the center of my laser spot, destroying the east wing of the building. We immediately turned outbound and set up for our second run-in. This bomb came off just as the first, and it guided precisely to the target, levelling the structure."

VF-103 continued supporting the counterinsurgency until November 2004 when they were relieved by Squadron VF-32 and its ten F-14Bs. By this time, VF-103 had flown 384 sorties and dropped twenty-one GBU-12s. Unfortunately for VF-32, the unit didn't see much action during its deployment—flying mostly presence patrols. In the summer of 2005, Squadrons VF-31 and VF-213 arrived in the Persian Gulf for what would be the final appearance of the F-14 Tomcat.

Taking off from the USS *Theodore Roosevelt* on February 8, 2006, pilots Captain William G. Sizemore from VF-213, and Lieutenant Bill Frank from VF-31, flew the final F-14 combat mission. The Tomcat squadrons that deployed in support of Operation Iraqi Freedom had flown a total of 1,163 combat sorties, logged 6,876 flight hours, and dropped 9,500 pounds of ordnance. On February 8, Lieutenant Frank became the last F-14 pilot to engage a hostile target in Iraq. He later noted, "We were called on to drop, and that's what we did. It's special and it's something I can say I did, but what's more important is the work of the Sailors who made it possible. They have worked so hard during this cruise to make every Tomcat operational."

After completing their mission, the pair of Tomcats bounded back to the *Theodore Roosevelt*. After Frank and Sizemore landed on the flight deck, Sizemore reflected on the poignancy of the moment. "It's the end of an era," he said. "This is one of the best airplanes ever built, and it's sad to see it go away. It's just a beautiful airplane. It's powerful, it has presence, and it just looks like the ultimate fighter." Months later, these F-14 crews began their transition to the F/A-18s.

Later, Vice Admiral Mike Malone, Commander Naval Air Forces Pacific, addressed the servicemen who had participated in the F-14 missions, stating:

"I want to congratulate each and every one of you for your performance in Operation Iraqi Freedom. You are demonstrating. . .that the United States has the greatest naval air power in the history of the world. Hostilities are still in progress, but Iraq has been liberated. Our president and country called upon you for your courage, dedication and skill. You responded with precise, persistent combat air power. We have seven aircraft carriers and air wings deployed in response to OIF. Each aircraft carrier is a sovereign piece of American territory—collectively, the most potent striking force ever assembled, and in working jointly with our allies, a remarkable testimony to our flexibility and capability."

It was a fitting end to a jet that fought long and hard for many years. By the time of its withdrawal from Iraqi airspace, and its subsequent retirement, the F-14 Tomcat had become one of the most respected fighting machines in military history.

Epilogue: Tomcat Sunset

Although the F-14 had proven itself during war and peacetime, Grumman Aerospace knew that the Tomcat would eventually outlive its utility. With this notion in mind, Grumman had embarked on numerous upgrades to the F-14 every few years. They needed to push the boundaries even further. Knowing that the full potential of the Tomcat hadn't been reached, Grumman grew more concerned over the emergence of McDonnell Douglas's F/A-18 series fighter. The US Navy, perennially on the lookout for a low-cost, agile, lightweight fighter, began putting more emphasis on the F/A-18 Hornet to fulfill the multi-role fighter/attack platform. Although the

Hornet was initially designed as a replacement for the A-6 Intruder, and a complement to the F-14, defense planners began eyeing the Hornet as a replacement for the aging Tomcat. Grumman, meanwhile, experimented with multiple concepts to keep the F-14 alive. But even the F-14D Quick Strike and Super Tomcat ST-21 concepts would not be enough to keep Grumman's champion from being sent to pastures.

Indeed, the changing needs of the US Navy, and the rejection of Grumman's multiple proposed improvements, were due in large part to the geopolitical changes of the post-Cold War era. Although the F/A-18 Hornet was on the rise, the Secretary of the Navy nonetheless agreed to participate with the Air Force in their Advanced Tactical Fighter (ATF) program in March 1986. Under the auspices of ATF, the Navy would create its own subset of the program called the Naval Advanced Tactical Fighter (NATF), chaired by Admiral Richard Dunleavy. The goal of both programs was to develop a common design that would simultaneously replace the F-14, F-15, and F-16. Hoping that the two military branches could achieve some commonality in their joint strike-fighter design, the Senate Armed Services Committee stated in 1987 that, "since the Navy must eventually replace the F-14 as well as the A-6, and the Air Force must eventually replace its F-111s along with its F-16s, the committee believes it is essential that the designs selected for the ATF and ATA [Advanced Tactical Aircraft] anticipate these additional cross-service requirements."

The Navy, however, had concerns throughout the process—mainly whether the final design would be suitable for carrier usage. Specific updates had to include, among other things: a stronger landing gear, a tail hook apparatus, and not surpass the size/weight limits of the carrier elevators and catapults. Due to these concerns, most of NATF's time and money went to ensure the feasibility of any Navy-specific alterations to the final design - including a maximum take-off weight of 65,000 pounds; a landing weight of 52,000 pounds; and spatial dimensions no bigger than the F-14 with its wings folded.

The ATF program continued into the early 1990s, eventually evolving into the Air Force's F-22 Raptor. The subsidiary NATF program, however, was less impressed with the F-22, deeming it unsuitable for carrier operations. Thus, in August 1990, Admiral Dunleavy halted the NATF program, noting that the F-22 alterations would be too costly. He further suggested that upgrading the F-14 would provide better results.

Secretary of Defense Dick Cheney, however, decided to halt production of the F-14 and subsequently upgrade the remaining Tomcats into the F-14D variant. This, of course, was a devastating blow to Grumman Aerospace and their Long Island facility, which employed nearly 25,000 people at the time. Faced with the pending loss of its F-14 assembly line, Grumman fought back. Over the next few months, the beleaguered aerospace company lobbied on Capitol Hill and ultimately enlisted the aid of Senators John Glenn and John McCain, both of whom were decorated military pilots.

After months of intense negotiation, the final outcome was deemed a "soft landing" for Grumman. Under this new bill, the older F-14s would still be upgraded to the D-variant specifications, but there would be additional funding for the purchase of newly-constructed F-14Ds. However, before receiving payment for these new fighter jets, Grumman had to sign an agreement to end the F-14D program and dismantle the assembly line upon completion of the new Tomcats. Virginia Senator John Warner noted he had "never seen such forceful, if not ruthless, lobbying" and nicknamed the F-14 terminating requirement the "poison pill."

Such was the beginning of the end for the F-14 Tomcat.

At the time, the US Navy had an active fleet of nearly 480 Tomcats. However, with its production halted, and Grumman Aerospace struggling to remain viable, the time was ripe for the F/A-18 to overtake its vaunted "big brother." Over the next decade, the Navy gradually phased out the Tomcat in favor of the lighter and leaner Hornet.

Influencing this decision was the geopolitical situation of the times. Soon after the Pentagon announced its decision to terminate production of the F-14, the Berlin Wall came down and the Soviet Union began to crumble from within. This turn of events soon raised serious questions about the future of America's defense policy. Specifically, could the Navy maintain its combat viability with fewer ships and lighter aircraft? Because the F-14 had been built to counter the Soviet threats that were now disintegrating, what should the future of naval aviation look like? Many believed the F/A-18 Hornet held the answer. It had a good combination of fighter and ground-attack capabilities, and its flight range could be extended to match those of the latter-day F-14s.

With the Cold War over, and the Navy re-evaluating the purpose of its fighter jets, the F-14 saw an adjustment in its usage and carrier numbers. As the Navy delivered more F/A-18s to their carrier squadrons, the number of F-14s gradually decreased. In 1993, for example, when Carrier Air Wing 11 embarked upon the USS *Abraham Lincoln* to participate in Operation Southern Watch (Iraq) and Operation Restore Hope (Somalia), they deployed with three F/A-18 squadrons, but only one squadron of F-14s. However, this high concentration of F/A-18s had proven effective for the Carrier Air Wing during its operations over Iraq and Somalia, thus facilitating the dissolution of other F-14 squadrons over the ensuing decade. Indeed, by 1997, no carrier air wing had more than one F-14 squadron in its ranks.

Meanwhile, Grumman worked hard to upgrade the existing fleet and complete delivery of the last D-variant Tomcats. The final F-14D was delivered to the Navy on July 20, 1992. Shortly thereafter, Grumman announced its departure from the business of military aviation. Then in April 1994, Grumman accepted a $2.17 billion merger from Northrop Aircraft, forming the current-day Northrop Grumman Corporation.

The newly-merged Northrop Grumman continued to support the existing fleet, but the need slowly dwindled as the millennium approached. The F-14 was scheduled to remain in service until 2008. But with the earlier "A" and "B" airframes being mothballed, and only a few D-variant squadrons still flying by 2006, the Department of Defense set the Tomcat's official retirement date for September 22, 2006.

The Tomcat's 2006 retirement ceremony was held at Naval Air Station Oceana in Virginia Beach, Virginia. More than 1,300 former F-14 aviators, maintainers, and support personnel were in attendance. By all accounts, it was a day filled with speeches and memories from the jet's illustrious 32-year history in American service. After the ceremony, the Tomcat had one final journey to make: Bethpage, New York, its final resting place. It was a fitting tribute for the last surviving Tomcat—returning to the birthplace of the original F-14.

The plane selected for display was the penultimate F-14D (Bureau Number 164603). The monument would stand in front of the Grumman building, for employees and visitors to admire for years to come. The ceremonial Tomcat left Naval Air Station Oceana on October 4, 2006 and, upon its arrival at Republic Airport in Farmingdale, New York, began its preparation for display by removing any critical internal parts.

This de-militarization process was necessary to keep those parts from falling into the hands of Iranian arms dealers, all of whom made black market purchases to maintain the IRIAF's ailing fleet of F-14s. In fact, the proliferation of latter-day F-14 parts became a major issue for the Pentagon. With no further Tomcats in production, and most of their spare parts having been expended, Iran became increasingly desperate to maintain its legacy fleet. Thus, knowing that the Iranian government would pay extortionate prices for F-14 parts, many arms dealers were now on the lookout for discarded Tomcat wares. In response, the Pentagon hired a St. Louis-based contractor, TRI-Rinse Inc., to destroy the remaining F-14s in the United States. Using a portable shredding machine, the company traveled to military bases across the country and shredded the F-14s on-site. As the founder of TRI-Rinse later remarked, "There were things [spare Tomcat parts] getting to the bad guys, so to speak. And one of the ways to make sure that no one will ever use an F-14 again is to cut them into little 2-by-2-foot bits."

With hundreds of F-14s being destroyed across the country—and the former Tomcat squadrons now flying the F/A-18—it seemed a bitterly anti-climactic end to the Navy's most famous fighter jet. From the chaff-filled skies over Iraq to the silver screens of Hollywood, the F-14 was more than just a stock military fighter. It had become a symbol of ingenuity and American air power. It was the silent protector with the ability to defend the skies by its presence alone. For more than three decades, the F-14 Tomcat delivered agile and aggressive firepower against America's enemies in the sky. Whatever the situation, or whatever the stakes, the Tomcat earned a formidable reputation among friend and foe alike.

That reputation endures today.

Select Bibliography

Adcock, Al. *F-14 Tomcat in Action*. Squadron Signal Publications, 1990.

Brown, Craig. *Debrief: A Complete History of U.S. Aerial Engagements 1981 to the Present*. Schiffer Pub, 2007.

Brown, David F. *Tomcat Alley: A Photographic Roll Call of the Grumman F-14 Tomcat*. Schiffer Pub, 1998.

Chant, Chris. *Air War in the Gulf 1991*. Osprey Publishing, 2001.

Cooper, Tom. "Persian Cats." *Air & Space Magazine*, Sept. 2006.

---- and Farzad Bishop. *Iranian F-14 Tomcat Units in Combat*. Osprey Publishing, 2012.

---- and Albert Grandolini. *Libyan Air Wars: Part 1: 1973-1985*. Helion and Company, 2015.

---- et al. *Libyan Air Wars: Part 2: 1985-1986*. Helion and Company, 2016.

---- et al. *Libyan Air Wars: Part 3: 1986-1989*. Helion and Company, 2016.

Gillcrist, Paul T. *Tomcat!: The Grumman F-14 Story*. Schiffer Pub, 1994.

Hallion, Richard. *Storm Over Iraq: Air Power and the Gulf War*. Smithsonian Institution, 2015.

Hildebrandt, Erik. *Anytime, Baby!: Hail and Farewell to the US Navy F-14 Tomcat*. Clear Hot Media, 2006.

Holmes, Tony. *F-14 Tomcat Units of Operation Enduring Freedom*. Osprey Publishing, 2012.

---- *Grumman F-14 Tomcat*. Haynes Publishing UK, 2018.

---- *US Navy F-14 Tomcat Units of Operation Iraqi Freedom*. Osprey Publishing, 2012.

Lake, Jon. *Grumman F-14 Tomcat: Shipborne Superfighter.* Airtime Pub, 1998.

Morse, Stan. *Gulf Air War: Debrief.* Airtime Pub, 1991.

Parsons, Dave, et al. *Grumman F-14 Tomcat: Bye - Bye Baby...!: Images & Reminiscences From 35 Years of Active Service.* Zenith Press, 2011.

Made in the USA
Middletown, DE
27 April 2020